"Morgan presents us with solid, well researched information on the Irish Morrigans from some of the best academic sources out there, and does it in a way that is engaging and approachable."
Segomâros Widugeni, previously known as **Aedh Rua**, author of *Celtic Flame: An Insider's Guide to Irish Pagan Tradition*

"*Pagan Portals: The Morrigan*, is a well-researched and heartfelt guide to the Morrigan from a fellow devotee and priestess. Morgan Daimler's impeccable scholarship and devotion to the Morrigan offers readers both sound historical resources as well as the author's personal experiences with this complex goddess. A perfect guide for those taking the first steps towards understanding the Morrigan."
Stephanie Woodfield, author of *Celtic Lore and Spellcraft of the Dark Goddess*

"There are so many faces of this amazing goddess and Daimler brings them together in a very readable way that enchanted me into turning page after page."
Elen Sentier, author of *Elen of the Ways* and *Trees of the Goddess*

"For those who seek the Morrigan and related goddesses, Morgan Daimler's short book packs a lot of information into a small space. Balancing historical information with modern insights and practices, it is an excellent text for new seekers and devotees. Each section of the book contains both the results of her reading and short discussions of her personal experience, giving it a valuable and much-needed balance between research and practice. I particularly enjoyed the section on her insights

about reconstructing seership practices with the goddess Badb."
Erynn Rowan Laurie, author of *A Circle of Stones* and *Ogam: Weaving Words of Wisdom*; co-author of the CR FAQs

Pagan Portals
The Morrigan
Meeting the Great Queens

Pagan Portals
The Morrigan
Meeting the Great Queens

Morgan Daimler

MOON
BOOKS

Winchester, UK
Washington, USA

JOHN HUNT PUBLISHING

First published by Moon Books, 2014
Moon Books is an imprint of John Hunt Publishing Ltd., No. 3 East Street, Alresford
Hampshire SO24 9EE, UK
office@jhpbooks.com
www.johnhuntpublishing.com
www.moon-books.com

For distributor details and how to order please visit the 'Ordering' section on our website.

Text copyright: Morgan Daimler 2014

ISBN: 978 1 78279 833 0
Library of Congress Control Number: 2014945005

A CIP catalogue record for this book is available from the British Library.

Design: Stuart Davies
www.stuartdaviesfineart.com

UK: Printed and bound by CPI Group (UK) Ltd, Croydon, CR0 4YY
Printed in North America by CPI GPS partners

We operate a distinctive and ethical publishing philosophy in all
areas of our business, from our global network of authors to
production and worldwide distribution.

CONTENTS

Dedicated to Macha, the Goddess I serve – may I always serve you well.

I'd like to thank everyone who inspired this book, especially the wonderful people of Morrigu's Daughters (and Sons). To Stephanie, Mayra, and Natalie, for helping me see the joy in service, and to Ivy and Melody, the Pine Cabin Crew, for letting me see the Morrigan through new eyes. To Ed, Michelle, Gina, Dawn, Jenna, and everyone else at the Morrigan's Call retreat. To Maya for constructive criticism and Allison for helpful suggestions.
To my husband Scott and my children Amara, Paige, and Terence for supporting me when I write with love, backrubs, and enforced computer breaks.

This book is for everyone who seeks the Morrigan and doesn't know where to start.

Author's Note

There are many very good books out there on the Morrigan, most of which are academic and some of which are very hard to find due to cost or age. People who are just finding themselves drawn to this increasingly popular but often enigmatic Goddess are left with a quandary; long, in-depth books which may be hard to get through on one hand, and a sea of questionable internet resources which are short and easier but often untrustworthy on the other. This book was written as a resource for seekers that will offer both solid academic material and anecdotes of connecting with the Morrigan in a format that is accessible and designed to be easy to read. It is meant to be a basic introduction to this Goddess and several closely related Goddesses by the same name, and also a bridge for beginners to feel more comfortable with the longer, more scholarly texts.

In writing this I have drawn on many different sources and have carefully referenced and cited all of them. My own degree is in psychology so I prefer to use the APA method of citations. This means that within the text after quotes or paraphrased material the reader will see a set of parenthesis containing the author's last name and date the source was published; this can then be cross references with the bibliography at the end of the book. I find this method to be a good one and I prefer it over footnotes or other methods of citation, which is why it's the one I use.

While this book can and does serve as a stand-alone work, ideally I hope that the reader will be drawn to learn more and decide to continue seeking. To help with this I have provided a list of both the references I used in my writing and also of recommended further reading at the end of the book under the bibliography. I have tried to offer books which represent an array of options for people with different viewpoints and approaches to honoring the Morrigan.

I do not think ultimately the framework we choose to use for our religion matters as much as that we make the effort to honor the old Gods and bring their worship into the modern world in ways that respect their history. I don't think a person has to follow a specific religion, be it Reconstructionist, Wiccan, or Celtic pagan, to do this if they are coming to the Gods with a sincere heart and good intent. To that end this book is written without any specific spiritual faith in mind, beyond polytheism, and it is up to the reader to decide how best to incorporate the material. However, my own religious path is Irish Reconstructionist polytheism and so that is bound to color some of my opinions in the text.

I have been an Irish pagan since 1991 and actively honoring the Morrigan since around 2000; I am a priestess of the Goddess Macha, often named as one of the Morrigans. I can say with certainty that her path isn't an easy one and it is one that will always push a person to keep learning and moving forward. In each chapter I am going to include a little section on my own personal experiences with the Morrigan, because I want to help people see that she is an active force in the world today and how we can honor her, beyond the bounds of any one faith. For some people this book may be the first step in a life-long journey. For others, perhaps, she doesn't call to you in that way, but nonetheless something valuable can be gained here, if only a greater understanding of the Goddess, her history, and modern beliefs and practices associated with her.

Introduction

The Morrigan was an important figure in Irish mythology and she is active still in the world today. She reaches out to us from the pages of the old myths, in the stories of the traditional story-tellers, and in modern songs. She comes to us on shadowed wings, in the still darkness, and in flashes of dreams. We hear her voice in the pounding of our own pulse, in the cry of the raven, and in the wild wind. She is a powerful force, but one that is often difficult to understand for those seeking her.

When we first feel the Morrigan's call we are confronted by a dizzying array of books and online sources purporting to teach us who she was and is. It quickly becomes clear though that the truth about the Morrigan is not so easily uncovered. Modern approaches to this ancient Goddess are often divorced from historic evidence of her; in contrast the older material can be harder to find and difficult to understand. Some put too much emphasis on personal experience while others ignore it. Ideally a modern seeker should try to find balance between all of these extremes.

There are several immediate challenges to face when we try to study the Morrigan. The first is understanding what her name itself means; not an easy thing because there is no clear answer. Next we have to understand that Morrigan is used as a name, a title, and a noun, so that we can find stories about the Morrigan – as well as the three Morrignae, or Morrigans, in English – about different named Goddesses being called Morrigan in certain contexts, and also about certain supernatural beings called morrigan. Seekers are also confronted with an array of traditional lore which is often contradictory and with concepts from ancient Ireland that have different meanings than we tend to think of, because they are coming from a different context, a different culture. All of these difficulties must be addressed at the very outset in order to move forward and learn about who the Morrigan was and to help understand her in a modern framework.

First let's look at the possible meanings of her name and see what each one can tell us about her character. The etymology of the name Morrigan is somewhat disputed, but the current leading theory is that it means, roughly, nightmare queen – often given as phantom queen – although others still prefer the once-popular "great queen" interpretation. The difference comes in depending on whether the first part of the name is given a fada (an accent mark in Irish which changes the sound of the vowel) and spelled Mor or Mór. Generally the accepted meaning of "Mor" is to relate it back to Old High German mara and Anglo-Saxon maere, meaning nightmare, although when accented, mór, it means great, large (eDIL, n.d.). Some people also try to relate mor to sea or ocean, thus rendering her name as meaning sea queen and tying her to the Morgan la Fey of Arthurian legend, but this is not widely accepted (eDIL, n.d.). Another theory is that mor relates to the Indo-European word móros, meaning death, and that the name means queen of the dead or queen of the slain (Gulermovich Epstein, 1998). The second part, rígan or rigan means queen or noble lady (eDIL, n.d.). Unfortunately there is no certainty on what the original meaning was. We can say though that the old Irish seems to have always been spelled Morrigan and likely did use the older meaning of nightmare queen, while the Mórrígan spelling was seen in the Middle Irish period along with the "great queen" interpretation. Looking at all of these together we see that her name could mean queen of phantoms, great queen, sea queen, or queen of the slain and each of these may hint at who she is and what she does.

The name is applied not only to a specific singular Goddess, but also to that deity's sisters, Badb and Macha. The Goddesses Fea and Nemain are also sometimes called Morrigan, and can be interchanged with the previous named Morrigan to form the different Morrigan triplicities. Personally I favor viewing the three Morrigans as Badb, Macha, and Morrigu and I am willing to accept Anand as the name of the Morrigan (this will be discussed in depth in the next chapter). It can be difficult at times to know whether we are talking about the individual Goddess who more often uses the title as her name or whether we are talking about a Goddess being given the title Morrigan. Sometimes context can be helpful here, but other times we can only guess and even the scholars don't agree in every situation. To complicate the issue further the word morrigan is used as a gloss, or translation, of the Greek word lamia and also is used in the same way for the word specters in some sources (Gulermovich Epstein, 1998). This means that when we look at the older material it is always best to be cautious when seeing the name Morrigan until context is understood.

Another problem that must be dealt with in studying the historic material relating to the Morrigan is that the old texts are often contradictory and include variations in the stories which can be significantly different. There are rarely single cohesive versions of any story, rather each one will have multiple versions, sometimes called redactions, which may have very different details. This means that what can seem a certainty in one version may be non-existent or contradicted in another. No single text should ever be read as if it were the authoritative version, but rather multiple redactions have to be read and then decisions made on the likeliest agreement of the information, that is what to be believed and what to be set aside. Nothing in Irish mythology or folklore is simple or straightforward, from genealogies to plot details, and often the deeper we look the muddier the picture becomes.

Finally a thoroughly modern problem of the Morrigan as an ancient Irish war Goddess is simply that we, as modern people, often don't understand what war was to the early Irish and hence what exactly a war Goddess was to them. Our modern wars are a far, far cry from the ancient battles and our society is structured in entirely different ways. While war has been and will always be a bloody, dangerous affair, war to the early Irish often revolved around cattle raids and involved small groups rather than huge armies as we would understand that concept today. Battle was done in a strictly honorable way, in equal combat often one-on-one or with matched armies, and we see this emphasized repeatedly in the old stories. Gulermovich Epstein in her dissertation *War Goddess: The Morrigan and her Germano-Celtic Counterparts* describes Irish martial practices as including: prediction of battle, incitement of the warriors, loud noise, direct attack, rejoicing in bloodshed, and declaring victory (Gulermovich Epstein, 1998). All of these are features common to the Morrigan when she is involved in warfare and demonstrate how she in many ways embodied the Irish practices of warcraft. The Morrigan is indeed a war Goddess, but her wars are played out in hand to hand – or more aptly sword to sword – combat, in the skill of a fighter against an opponent, in the cleverness of the cattle raid, in courage and skill and the will to win.

Understanding the Morrigan is a process. It involves understanding the individual Goddesses called Morrigan as much as understanding the Morrigu herself. It means understanding her different roles in mythology and the importance of the forms she can assume. And it means understanding how all of the historical material ties in to modern worship and shapes her place in the modern world.

Chapter One

Morrigu – Goddess of Battle

Badb and Macha, greatness of wealth, Morrigu
springs of craftiness,
sources of bitter fighting
were the three daughters of Ernmas.
(Macalister, 1941)

The name Morrigan is a title, but is also used as a personal name usually prefaced by "the". It appears in various forms including Morrigu, Morrigna, and Morrighan; the modern Irish is Mórríoghain. When all three of the Goddesses who share the title Morrigan are being referred to together you will see it as Morrignae, although for the purpose of this work I will gloss that as Morrigans.

Historic Material

In the Lebor Gabala Erenn we are told: *"Delbaeth... has three daughters, the famous war-furies Badb, Macha, and Mórrígu, the latter sometimes called Anand or Danand."* (Macalister, 1941). She is the daughter of Ernmas according to the same text: *"Ernmas had other daughters, Badb, and Macha, and Morrigu, whose name was Anand."* (Macalister, 1941). Her mother, Ernmas, is called both a farmer and a sorceress of the Tuatha De Danann and her father, Delbaeth, is one of the kings of the Gods. This potentially ties her into different aspects of sovereignty and magic through her parentage. We also know from this that her two sisters are Badb and Macha, themselves also called Morrigan in different places, and all three together are called an trí Morrignae, the three Morrigans. She has three other sisters as well, Banba, Fotla, and Eriu, the three sovereignty Goddesses of Ireland.

The material from the Lebor Gabala Erenn tells us that the Morrigan's name could actually be Anand or Danand (or Anu or Danu[1]) and indeed both are given as her name in various portions of the text (Macalister, 1941). For example, in verse 62, she is listed as one of the sisters with Badb and Macha: "*Badb and Macha and Anand, of whom are the Paps of Anu in Luachar, were the three daughters of Ernmas the she-farmer.*" (Macalister, 1941). When the Anu connection is accepted some people further relate her to Aine who we will discuss in a later chapter (Berresford Ellis, 1987; Jones, 2009). The connection to Danu is based on the idea that Anu and Danu are the same Goddess; this would make her the ultimate progenitor or matriarch of the Tuatha Dé Danann. A single portion of the Lebor Gabala Erenn says: "*The Morrigu, daughter of Delbaeth, was the mother of the other sons of Delbaeth, Brian, Iucharba, and Iuchair: and it is from her additional name 'Danann' the Paps of Ana in Luachair are called, as well as the Tuatha De Danann.*" (Macalister, 1941).

However, it should be noted that in multiple sources including the Cath Maige Tuired, Morrigan and Danand are listed separately; making it unlikely that Danu or Danand is one of the Morrigans. Indeed Danand is the daughter of the Goddess Flidais according to one version of the LeBór Gabala Erenn, not a child of Ernmas (Macalister, 1941). The evidence for Anu or Anand is stronger and more persuasive, but Anu herself is an obscure Goddess; the Sanas Cormaic says that she, Anand, is the mother of the Irish Gods (Jones, 2009). It is probable that Anand may be the name of the Morrigu, but I find the evidence connecting her to Danand much less solid. Part of the reason for this is that the names Anand and Danand have different meanings, "abundance" and "flowing" respectively, which make it seem far more likely that the two were separate Goddesses later conflated due to the similarity in their names. It is also likely, in my opinion, that some of the variations and confusion reflect different regional beliefs later fused together when the stories were written down.

Relationships

Morrigu is sometimes said to be the wife of the Dagda. In the Book of Lecan we are told: "*Anand .i. in Morrigan... bean aile do'n Dagda,*" meaning: "Anand, that is the Morrigan... is the wife of the Dagda" (Heijda, 2007). She is said to have had a daughter, Adair, by the Dagda, and 26 daughters and 26 sons who were all warriors by an unnamed father or fathers (Gray, 1983; Gulermovich Epstein, 1998). In fairness to different viewpoints some people do interpret these 52 warriors not as physical children but as people dedicated to her.

Possibly her most well-known child is her son, Meche, by an unnamed father. Meche had three serpents in his heart, which could have destroyed all of Ireland, so he was killed and his heart burned; the ashes were put in a river where they killed all the animal life (Gray, 1983). According to the invasion myths she had three sons, Glon, Gaim, and Coscar, by an unknown father and three other sons, Brian, Iucharba, and Iuchair, by her own father Delbaeth (Macalister, 1941).

Forms

The Morrigan has many forms. She often appears as a crow or raven and is well known for taking this shape. In the Táin Bó Cúailgne, and possibly the story of Da Derga's Hostel, she appears as a heifer, and in many myths she is associated with stealing cattle. She can be a beautiful young woman or a terrifying old hag, a bird, a wolf, an eel, or a cow. She appears in the air, on land, and in the water. Unlike many other Irish deities she is explicitly referred to as a Goddess at least twice in the historic material and we have one ancient prayer to her. In the prayer she is being called on by a man who says she had previously been good to him and is asking for her help in gaining a herd of cattle (Gulermovich Epstein, 1998).

Associations

The Morrigan is a Goddess with many skills and powers. She appears to both the Dagda and to Cu Chulain offering victory if they have sex with her; one agrees and one refuses. In the Táin Bó Cúailgne, Cu Chulain spurns her amorous advances and she sets herself against him; the two fight and he deals her three wounds, which she later tricks him into healing. In the Cath Maige Tuired, she unites with the Dagda and after lying with him promises to fight alongside the Tuatha Dé Danann in the coming battle.

In mythology, the Morrigan aids the Tuatha Dé Danann in fighting against both the Fir Bolg and the Fomorians by using magic to shower fire, blood and fog upon the enemy and to weaken or kill one of the opposing kings (Gray, 1983; O hOgain, 2006). Indeed, in these battles she uses both magic and physical battle to defeat the enemy of the Tuatha Dé Danann. The second battle of Maige Tuired lists the three Morrigans as Druids, and the Banshenchas lists them as witches (Gray, 1983; Banshenchas, n.d.). She appeared before the battle of Mag Rath as a thin, gray-haired old woman who flew over the battlefield and leapt from spear point to shield rim of the soldiers who would win the battle during the fight (Smyth, 1988).

The Morrigan is associated with war, battle, and death, certainly, but also with victory, strategy, magic, and possibly sovereignty. She can give courage or take it away. She is a Goddess of glory in battle and the cleverness of the cattle raid, which was an essential aspect of early Irish society. Several authors posit that her connection to cattle relates to her role as a sovereignty Goddess. O hOgain goes the furthest in suggesting she is a land Goddess and a mother Goddess through her possible connection to Danu (O hOgain, 2006).

Although it is unlikely that she is a mother Goddess by even a loose definition of the term she does seem to have sovereignty qualities as a Goddess who influences battles and therefore decides the outcomes of wars and kingship disputes. She often appears near or in connection with rivers, which might support the idea of her as a Goddess connected to water, and her association with the Paps of Anu, breast-shaped hills in County Kerry, and other locations may support her connection as a land Goddess. I tend to reject that association myself, but leave it up to the reader to decide for themselves based on the evidence. Her strongest associations are clearly with warfare and also with fate so that some people have connected her to the Norse Valkyries (Jones, 2009; Gulermovich Epstein, 1998).

Several locations are named for the Morrigan including the whirlpool of Corryveckan, which is sometimes called the Morrigan's Cauldron. The river ford known as the "Bed of the Couple" is named for her Samhain tryst with the Dagda. Gort na Morrigna, field of the Morrigan, in county Louth is hers as is Fulacht na Morrigna, Morrigan's Hearth, in county Tipperary (Smyth, 1988). In the Bóyne valley Mur na Morrigna, mound of the Morrigan, is also hers as well as Da Chich na Morrigna, the Paps of the Morrigan (Smyth, 1988; O hOgain, 2006). The cave of Cruachan, also called Uaimh na gCait or Oweynagat (cave of cats), is especially associated with her and is the site of another of her cattle stealing episodes.

Poem for the Morrigan

She is blood and battle and death
The blade that cleaves flesh from bone
That cuts the old from the new
That reshapes, remakes, redefines us
Blood is not to be feared; it is the current of life
Battle is not to be feared; it is the price of sovereignty
Death is not to be feared; it is the end of the old...
And a new beginning, endlessly

An Offering Prayer to Anu

Great Battle Queen

Anu of the Tuatha De Danann
Called Morrigu
Who promises to deliver
Two handfuls of your enemy's blood
Who promises to catch what is chased
And kill what is captured
Mighty Anu of the people of skill
Accept this offering from me

Invocation to the Morrigan

Queen of battle,
Queen of war
Shape-shifting woman
Raven, wolf, and heifer
Bathing in bloodshed
Offering life or death
Obscurity or glory
Strong shield and
sharp spear point
Morrigan
I call to you

The Morrigan in My Life

I believe the Morrigan respects physical and martial skill and so
am seeking to honor her in those ways as best I can; as part of this
I am working on training in self-defense and basic martial skills.
I created a small shrine to her that includes images of her animal
forms and have been meditating on what each one represents, as
well as the connection between her and war, death, battle, victory,
strategy, magic, and sovereignty. I think it is possible that Anand
may be connected to some aspect of mothering, but I see her as
the defensive and protective aspects of mothering not the
nurturing ones; she is the snarling wolf willing to rip the throat
out of anything to protect her puppies, just as Morrigu fought to

protect the Tuatha De Danann from the Fir Bolg and Fomorians. As we can see from her stories, she is a Goddess who expects a price to be paid for her blessing; nothing with her is free or easy.

My experiences with the Morrigan under the name Anu have been interesting. I find her energy to be very deep and solid, reminiscent of a standing stone. There is an immensity to her that is hard to describe, but decidedly numinous to experience. I see her as an intense younger woman with dark hair and a slim form, but to me she also had an oddly hooded or shadowed appearance, as if what I was seeing wasn't entirely set or decided.

Chapter Two

Macha – Goddess of Sovereignty

Machæ: an tres morrīgan, unde mesrad Machæ .i. cendæ doine iarna n-airlech.
Macha: the third Morrigan; Macha's crop: the heads of slaughtered men
O'Mulconry's Glossary, 8th century (Jones, 2008)

Macha's name is connected to crows, cattle, pastures and fields. It's possible that her name may mean plain or field (Sjoedstedt, 2000). The electronic dictionary of the Irish language lists several meanings for the word in Old Irish including Royston (hooded) crow, milking yard/field, and field or plain. In modern Irish the word means cattle field or yard, a fine group of cattle in a pasture, or, when added to brea bó, a herd (O Donaill, 1977).

Historic Material

Macha is one of the Tuatha Dé Danann who appears in several different places in Irish mythology. She is a daughter of Ernmas, sister to Badb and Anand; these three sisters make up the triple Morrigan. In some sources Macha herself is called Morrigan; specifically in the Book of Femroy Macha is given as another name for the Morrigan, *"Macha .i. in Morrigan"*, Macha, that is, the Morrigan (O hOgain, 2006; Heijda, 2007).

Macha is also referred to as Badb, given the name as a title in the same way she is called Morrigan (Coe, 1995). Although some people feel that only the Macha of the Tuatha Dé Danann is the Macha who is of the Morrigan others, myself included, feel that she appears several times in myth under the same name, but in different roles. There are also those who will argue that Macha herself is not the Morrigan at all, but a related deity with some overlapping functions. This chapter will present information on all the appearances of Macha and as usual leave it up to the reader to draw conclusions.

Macha appears in different guises in Irish mythology: as one of the daughters of Partholon, as one of the Nemedians, as one of the Tuatha Dé Danann, as a "fairy woman" and as a queen. This last one may or may not represent a pseudo-historic queen or a story about the Goddess. There is debate among modern followers of the Morrigan on this topic because the story has mythic overtones, but is not explicitly mythic, unlike her other appearances. However, many scholars do see Macha the queen as connected to the Goddess, as do I.

Macha Daughter of Partholon
In the first appearance of Macha she is listed in the Lebor Gabala Erenn as one of the daughters of Partholon. Nothing more is said about her and nothing is known about her from this story except that it can be assumed she dies with all her people during a plague. Interestingly, however, we should note that the meaning of the name Partholon might be son of the ocean and when we see Macha later in the story of Macha the fairy woman she lists her lineage as coming from the son of the ocean (Jones, 2008). This could be sign of the continuity between the different Macha stories.

Macha of the Nemedians
In the second story she appears as the wife of Nemed, of the third race to settle Ireland, and is said to die clearing the plains of Ireland for farming (Macalister, 1941). In alternative versions her husband cleared the land and he named it for her after she died. It was also said she had a vision of the future Táin Bó Cúailgne and the destruction and carnage it would cause and died of a broken heart (Green, 1992). Because she died clearing the land for farming she is associated with the earth and its

produce. The connection of the meaning of her name to cows and milking as well as fields and pasture, I think, also supports the view of her as a land Goddess. Interestingly John Carey in his essay "Notes on the Irish War Goddess" describes this Macha as both a seeress and a war Goddess, or woman who practices war magic (Coe, 1995).

Macha of the Tuatha Dé Danann

She appears in the Lebor Gabala Erenn among the Tuatha Dé Danann where she is called a daughter of Ernmas (Macalister, 1941). Several modern authors including Berresford Ellis and Jones suggest she was the wife of Nuada Argatlamh, king of the Tuatha Dé Danann, himself a complex deity, probably because the two are paired in battle and death in the Cath Maige Tuired and Lebor Gabala Erenn. This has become a popular belief and it is one I personally embrace as well, although the reader may form their own opinion. There is some supposition that it was Macha as Morrigan who joined with the Dagda a year before the second battle of Maige Tuired (Berresford Ellis, 1987).

In the Lebor Gabala Erenn it says: *"Délbaeth... has three daughters, the famous war-furies Badb, Macha, and Mórrígu..."* (Macalister, 1941). In this appearance she is killed in the second battle of Maige Tuired, but Macalister in one section of his notes on the Lebor Gabala Erenn volume IV says that it is logical to believe that this Macha and the fairy woman Macha who curses the men of Ulster are in fact the same being. Macalister also posits that the Morrigan was not originally a triplicity, and that Macha joined an existing Badb/Anand pairing, because Macha had her own center of worship at Armagh and he believes the genealogies suggest an earlier tradition to which Macha was later added (Macalister, 1941).

This provides us a variety of interesting information about Macha. We learn that she is the daughter of Delbaeth and Ernmas, who we have previously discussed, and sister to Badb and Anand, and is one of the three Morrigans. We learn as well that her husband may be Nuada the king (twice) of the Gods and that she fights and dies with him in battle. We also learn through Macalister's commentary that it is likely that Macha originally had her own separate cult centered in Ulster, which over time merged with an existing cult of Badb and Morrigu to form the Morrigan triplicity we know today.

In the Cath Maige Tuired it is also hinted that she actually takes the battlefield, as she does in the Lebor Gabala Erenn, because it mentions her along with Badb and Morrigu accompanying the warriors to the battle. In the Banshenchas she is listed as one of the Tuatha Dé Danann's magic workers, listed either as witches or sorceresses. In the first battle of Mag Tuired she acts with the other two Morrigans to use magic against the enemy by sending rain, fog, and showers of blood and fire upon the opposing army. The second battle of Mag Tuired lists the three Morrigans as ban-draoithe, or Druids (Gray, 1983). This tells us that not only is she a warrior but also a magic user, especially of battle magic, in support of the side she is on.

Macha the Fairy Woman

Next she appears as a fairy woman in the prelude to the Táin Bó Cúailgne and marries a farmer or chieftain named Crunnuic (often given as Crunnchu); she appears in his home and acts the part of his wife without initially speaking a word to him, eventually becoming pregnant with twins. He goes to a festival held by the king who is boasting of the speed of his chariot horses. Crunnuic, despite being warned by Macha not to speak of her to anyone else, brags that his wife could outrace the king's horses, and the furious king demands that Crunnuic bring her immediately to race or forfeit his life. Macha is brought to the assembly, but begs for a delay as she is in labor. Despite her pleas she is denied her request and forced to race anyway. She wins, collapsing and birthing her twins just past the finish line, then curses the men of Ulster with nine days of labor pain in their greatest hour of need for nine times nine generations, before dying. In some versions of the story she doesn't die, but simply returns to the Otherworld, because Crunnuic broke her prohibition against speaking of her[2].

According to the Metrical Dindshenchas, Macha gives birth to a boy and girl named Fír and Fíal (Gwynn, 1924). Interestingly, possible meanings of the name Fír include true, a pledge, a test or an ordeal, and Fíal means faithfully, seemly, or decorous, so that Macha's two children could possibly have names meaning "true" and "faithfully". Although this is entirely speculative based on the word meanings in Old Irish, it does seem quite fitting given the story they appear in. Indeed, one translation of the Rennes Dindshenchas gives her children's names as Truth and Honor (Coe, 1995).

To this day the spot of the race and the twin's birth carries her name, Emain Macha, where for a long time festivals and assemblies were held, especially at Lughnasa (McNeill, 1962). It is from this story that her associations with horses, childbirth, pregnancy, and, again, the produce of the earth – by marrying a farmer – are seen. There are several details that also connect her subtly to sovereignty as well; the horses she races are both white, a sacred color, and she herself is equated to the sun, land, and sea (Coe, 1995).

The Rennes Dindshenchas connects this Macha, Macha of the Nemedians, and the Macha of the Tuatha Dé Danann because all three are referenced in the same poetic entry. It is also important to note that the curse laid on the men of Ulster by this Macha is essential to the great Irish epic the Táin Bó Cúailgne, in which the Morrigan plays a significant role and which we will discuss in more depth in a later chapter.

Macha Mog Ruadh

In the final story we see her connection to sovereignty and battle.

Lady of the Holy People
I call to you
Warrior and Druidess
Wielder of fierce magic
Queen of the Tuatha De
I call to you
Sun of womanhood
Swifter than steeds
· Lady of the Sí
I call to you

Each verse above could be used as a stand-alone with the first line if preferred.

The Morrigan in My Life

I have found Macha to be fiercely loving and protective of those she calls her own, with a strong maternal energy to her, but she can be very no-nonsense and unbending as well. She always appears to me as a red-haired warrior woman wearing a cloak of black feathers and riding or walking next to a black or white horse, sometimes both. To me she is a Goddess of the sovereignty of the land, a protector of the weak, and Goddess of women and women's issues, especially pregnancy and childbirth. She is also battle and pride and the will to win, and her spirit is the warrior's spirit.

Because horse races were a common event at Lughnasa celebrations and because such celebrations were held at that time at her sacred places, especially Emain Macha, I tend to associate that holiday with her in particular. In one version of the Dindshenchas we are told that on Mag Macha, Macha's Plain, there were memorial fairs held for her, called Oenach Macha (Coe, 1995). These fairs and the reason for them are strongly reminiscent of Lughnasa as well and reinforce her probable connection to that holiday.

Chapter Three

Badb – Goddess of Prophecy

Delbaeth... has three daughters, the famous war-furies Badb, Macha, and Mórrígu, the latter sometimes called Anand or Danand. (Macalister, 1941).

The name Badb is very difficult to define and its etymology is complicated and contested. Some sources trace it back to the root bodvo, which means crow, while others tie it in to buduo meaning battle; a third option relates it to bhedh, which means to stab or cut (Heijda, 2007). All of these possible root meanings have strong points and relate to different aspects of the Goddess Badb. The eDIL describes the word Badb as being both the name of a Goddess and meaning *"Scald-crow; deadly; fatal; dangerous; ill-fated; warlike; venomous"* (eDIL, n.d.).

Scald crow is another name for the hooded crow, or Caróg liath in Irish (corvus cornix), a type of crow that is predominantly gray with black wings and head, giving a hooded appearance. This crow is a form taken by the Morrigan and in particular by Badb. Badb is also spelled Badhbh or Bodb and may be pronounced Bayv or Bibe. I favor pronouncing it Bayv, which goes with the Badhbh spelling. She may also be called Badb Catha, or battle crow and some people suggest a connection between her and the Gaulish Cathbodua.

Historic Material

Badb is the daughter of Delbaeth and Ernmas, sister to Macha and Morrigu/Anann, and is said to have two children, Ferr Doman and Fiamain (Macalister, 1941; Gray, 1983). In the Banshenchas she is said to be the wife of the Dagda. This might be why people sometimes identify her as the Morrigan who slept

Chapter Four

The Morrigan by Other Names

Nemain

Nemain, Danand, Badb and Macha, Morrigu who brings victory, impetuous and swift Etain, Be Chuilli of the north country, were the sorceresses of the Tuatha De.
(Banshenchus, n.d.)

Nemain, also called Neman, Nemon, or Nemhain, is probably the other Goddess most often included as one of the three Morrigans. Her name possibly means venomous or frenzy (Berresford Ellis, 1987; Green, 1992). However, the etymology is highly speculative and uncertain. In many modern popular books she can be found listed along with Badb and Macha as the three Morrigan, as if she were the Morrigu. Hennessey in his 1870 book *The Ancient Irish Goddess of War* seems to have been the first to say that the Morrigan triplicity consisted of Badb, Macha, and Nemain, something that has often been repeated since. The quote from the Banshenchus above, however, demonstrates the older view clearly did not see her as the Morrigu, although she might have born the title of Morrigan as did Badb. Indeed, in the stories where Nemain appears she is most often paired with Badb alone and seems to act as a battle Goddess in her own right, separate from the three Morrigans who we often see acting together elsewhere.

Nemain is said to be the daughter of Elcmar, the original owner of Brugh na Bóyne and possibly an alternate name of Nuada. She is the sister of Fea and wife of Neit, an obscure God of war, although the phrase Bé Neit, which is translated wife of Neit, can also mean woman of war or battle and appears elsewhere as a name in its own right. To add to the confusion on this issue some sources describe her as the wife of Nuada and conflate her with Macha, while others describe her as an aspect of Badb (Berresford Ellis, 1987; O hOgain, 2006). In one source she is called beautiful and described as a judge (Gulermovich Epstein, 1998). All descriptions of her mention battle and war.

Nemain is associated with battle frenzy and exciting or terrifying armies. Her name itself is sometimes translated in the old texts as a word meaning battle fury or frenzy, and like Badb can be used to mean witch (Heidja, 2007). In the Táin Bó Cúailgne she appears twice, once to terrify Medb's army at night, and a second time when Cu Chulain cries out in fury Nemain appears and wreaks havoc among the opposing army, causing the men to kill each other in confusion and fear (Hennessey, 1870). In the Táin Bó Cúailgne she raises such a terrifying cry that 100 warriors die at hearing it. As mentioned above the Banshenchas lists her as a magic worker among the Tuatha Dé Danann, and the Lebor Gabala Erenn describes her as *"Neman of ingenious versicles[5]"* (Banshenchus, n.d.; Macalister, 1941).

Her place among the Morrigans is somewhat uncertain. It is clear in the Invasion texts that she was seen as separate from the three daughters of Ernmas, Badb, Macha, and Morrigu, although in later mythological cycles she does often appear acting with Badb or associated with her. As Gulermovich Epstein says, *"What is not clear is whether Nemain was actually considered one of the morrigna by the medieval Irish literati since most of the evidence... is circumstantial. However if [we use morrigan as a general term] it seems appropriate to include Nemain in that group."* (Gulermovich Epstein, 1998).

Prayer to Nemain

Nemain
Furious, frenzied,
Screaming in battle

Laying low strong warriors
Nemain
Wife of War
Beautiful judge
Who knows no fear
Nemain
Help me find strength
Help me overcome fear
Help me be true to myself

Fea

Fea and Neman, the two wives of Net son of Indiu, two daughters of Elcmar of the Brug.
(Macalister, 1941).

Her name may mean hateful, in fact Cormac's glossary goes so far as to define it as meaning all things hateful (Berresford Ellis, 1987; Heijda, 2007). Other authors, however, relate it to the Irish words fee and fé, which mean death and a measuring rod for the grave, and possibly back to the Latin *vae* meaning an exclamation of woe (Gulermovich Epstein, 1998). As with Nemain though the etymology is uncertain and Fea is an obscure Goddess who we know very little about. She is said to be a sister of Nemain; both are daughters of Elcmar and both are wives of Neit according to the Lebor Gabala Erenn. Both Fea and Nemain in some of the genealogies are the nieces of the three previously named Morrigans (Gulermovich Epstein, 1998).

Fea is obscure, but seems to have been most strongly associated with south Leinster, especially Mag Fea, the plain of Fea, which bears her name (Heijda, 2007). Interestingly, Fea also has an association with cattle, as does the Morrigan. In the Dindshenchas she is connected to two oxen, Fe and Men; the same passage describes her as "silent" and "beloved"

(Gulermovich Epstein, 1998).

Bé Neit

Another obscure battle Goddess associated with the Morrigan is Bé Neit, whose name can be translated as either wife of Neit or woman of battle. In one version of the Táin Bó Cúailgne Badb and Nemain appear along with Bé Neit to harass the Connacht army at night. There is very little information on this Goddess, and indeed Heijda in her dissertation "War Goddesses, Scald Crows, and Furies" suggests that the identification of Bé Neit as a separate being is a scribal error and should actually say "*Badb, who is the wife of Net, and Nemain*", rather than listing them as three individuals. Other sources list Bé Neit as Nemain, while still others say she is the Morrigan (Gulermovich Epstein, 1998). In one text we find out that Bé Neit was believed to have power over the outcomes of battles, "*...upon which of them battle-mourning Bé Neit would establish her mighty power (and so gain them the victory)*" (Gulermovich Epstein, 1998). It is possible that Bé Neit was meant to be understood as meaning woman of battle and could be used to describe any of the war Goddesses, rather than being a proper name.

Áine – or Anu?

In some modern mythology Áine (pronounced Awn-yuh or Awn-uh) is seen as an aspect of Anu or the Morrigan (Berresford Ellis, 1987). Lady Gregory, writing in 1904, stated that some people in Ireland believed that Áine "was the Morrigu herself" showing that there was an old folk belief connecting the two (Gregory, 1904). However, while Anu's name means abundant, Áine's name is related to shining and brightness indicating a basic difference in the two deities; they also have very little mythology in common or that could be seen as similar. Interestingly, Grian, who we will also discuss, is seen as a possible aspect of Macha, probably due to a reference to Macha in the Metrical

Dindesenchas that gives an epithet of Grian to her. While I disagree with these associations, I admit that I find it fascinating that Áine and Grian are strongly associated with each other and a possible division of the year, and each is also associated with the Morrigan and Macha respectively. I will give the reader what we know of Áine historically and leave it up to the reader to decide whether the connection to the Morrigan has any weight to it.

It's an interesting thing in Irish mythology and folklore that the Gods were reduced not into human characters, by and large, but into fairies. So it is with Áine of Cnoc Áine in county Kerry, who is believed to have been a Goddess originally, but is held to be a Lady of the Sí now with the fairy hill of Knockainy being her special place. In Irish belief this is because after humans came to Ireland the Gods went into the sí, the hollow hills, and became the aos sí, the people of the fairy hills. This later evolved into seeing the Tuatha Dé Danann as part of the beings of Fairy, but because the modern – especially modern American – idea of what fairies are is so different from the traditional concepts this can cause confusion. The Gods are still the Gods, even in the sí, and it is a mistake to minimize them into twee little things because it's trendy to see fairies that way now. As to the idea of Gods as fairies my own view is that it doesn't really matter whether a being is a God in every story or sometimes appears as a fairy, as I see beings as on a scale of power where a powerful enough fairy and a God within a sí are effectively the same thing under different terms. It's sort of a po-tay-to/pah-tah-to situation where the label is incidental to the actual being.

Like most Irish deities, Áine has a complex and sometimes contradictory mythology. She is said in some sources to be the daughter of Manannan Mac Lir and in others to be the daughter of Manannan's foster son Eogabail, a Druid of the Tuatha Dé Danann (Berresford Ellis, 1987). No mother is listed for her. Some sources say that her sister is Finnen, whose name means white

31

(Monaghan, 2004). Her name likely means brightness or splendor and she is often associated with the sun (O hOgain, 2006; Monaghan, 2004). In fact not far from her hill of Cnoc Áine is another hill, Cnoc Gréine, associated with the Goddess Grian who is also reputed be a fairy queen; MacKillop suggests the two Goddesses might represent the summer and winter suns respectively and some sources list them as sisters (MacKillop, 1998; Monaghan, 2004).

In much of her later folklore Áine is reputed to have love affairs with mortals and several Irish families claim descent from her. The most well-known of these human descendants is the third Earl of Desmond, Gearoid Iarla. It is said by some that Gearoid did not die but was taken into Loch Guirr and would return one day (Berresford Ellis, 1987). Other tales say that he still lives within the lake and can be seen riding beneath the water on a white fairy horse, while still other stories claim that Áine turned him into a goose on the shore of the lake (Berresford Ellis, 1987). She was also said to have been raped by the king Aillil Olom, on Samhain, who stories say she either bit off an ear from, or she killed in punishment (Monaghan, 2004; Berresford Ellis, 1987; O hOgain, 2006). The child of this union was Eogan whose line went on to claim rulership of the land through their descent from the Goddess (Monaghan, 2004).

Áine is associated with fertility, agriculture, sovereignty, and the sun, as well as love (Berresford Ellis, 1987; Monaghan, 2004). She is especially connected to red mares, with some people claiming she could assume this form (MacKillop, 1998; Monaghan, 2004). She may also be associated more generally with horses and possibly with geese and sheep as they appear in her folklore. The hill of Cnoc Áine is one of the most well-known places connected with her, said to have been named after her during the settling of Ireland when she used magic to help her father win the area (O hOgain, 2006).

Midsummer was her special holy day and up until the 19th

century people continued to celebrate her on the eve of midsummer with a procession around the hill, carrying torches of burning straw in honor of Áine na gClair, Áine of the Wisps (Berresford Ellis, 1987). Áine is also sometimes called Áine Chlair, a word that may relate to wisps or may be an old name for the Kerry or Limerick area (Monaghan, 2004; O hOgain, 2006). On midsummer clumps of straw would be lit on her hill and then scattered through the cultivated fields and among the cows to propitiate Áine's blessing (O hOgain, 2006). In county Louth there is a place called Dun Áine where people believe that the weekend after Lughnasa belongs to Áine, and in some folklore she is said to be the consort of Crom Cruach during the three days of Lughnasa (O hOgain, 2006; MacNeill, 1962). Additionally there is another hill called Cnoc Áine in county Derry, and a third in Donegal (O hOgain, 2006). In Ulster there is a well called Tobar Áine that bears her name.

Whether a Goddess or fairy queen, Áine has been much loved, even up until fairly recently. Her mythology is convoluted but fascinating and any who feel the need or desire to honor a solar Goddess within an Irish framework would do well to learn more about Áine. As they say, she is "The best hearted woman who ever lived" (O hOgain, 2006).

Invocation to Áine

Queen of the sí of Cnoc Áine
Red mare who circles the lake
Lady of Midsummer bonfires
of straw torches and burning wisps
Áine of the harvest
Áine of the summer sun
Áine of the fairy hill
I call to you

Grian – Another Name for Macha?

Grian (roughly pronounced Gree-uhn) is an obscure Irish Goddess whose mythology is lost to us. She is not mentioned in any of the surviving stories or myths, except in brief references as Áine's sister. Grian appears in folklore as the queen of a sí, Cnoc Greine, as well as a lake, Loch Greine or Lough Graney, both in county Limerick (Berrisford Ellis, 1987; Smyth, 1988). Cnoc Greine is about seven miles from Knockainey, the sí of Áine (Smyth, 1988). In folklore Grian is said to be a sister of Áine and daughter of Fer I (Yew man), but little else is known about her family or relationships. Some authors including MacKillop and Smyth suggest that Grian may be an aspect of Áine, or another name for her, although I don't favor that idea myself.

The word grian, with a fada over the i, means sun, bright, radiant, sunny-faced, sunny, and meeting place; the word grian without the fada means sand, sea, river, base, foundation, earth, and land (eDIL, n.d.). Both meanings are intriguing to contemplate, although the generally accepted meanings connected to the name Grian relate to the sun. Grian is widely thought to be a sun or solar Goddess in a similar way to Áine. It may be possible that the connection to Áine is based on an older belief that Áine represented the strong summer sun, while Grian represented the more distant winter sun; in this way each sister would have been seen to rule over part of the year by controlling the sun during that time (MacKillop, 2008). With Áine's connection to midsummer celebrations it is possible that Grian would once have been honored at the winter solstice (MacKillop, 2008; Monaghan, 2004). This could be compared to the modern division of the year into a dark and light half at these times, and to the stories of the Oak and Holly Kings in neopaganism or the Scottish folk belief (also likely modern) of Brighid and the Cailleach sharing the year.

There may also be a connection between Grian and Macha that is worth considering as well. In the Metrical Dindshenchas it is said that Macha's other name is Grian: "*...her two names, not seldom heard in the west, were bright Grian and pure Macha*" and "*...in the west she was Grian, the sun of womankind.*" (Gwynn, 1924). Some suggest that Grian was used at times as an epithet and that this may be the case with Macha being called the sun of womankind (Monaghan, 2004). Unfortunately there is nothing else referencing this connection in other sources outside the Dindshenchas that I am aware of, but taken with Áine's possible connection to the Morrigan it would not be unreasonable to accept.

While our information about Grian is scarce there is enough to give us a basic understanding of her as a Goddess connected to the sun who likely balanced the year with her sister Áine. Any association with Grian and the winter solstice is based on supposition, but that supposition is logical. Similarly the connection of Áine and Grian to the Morrigan sisterhood, while more tenuous, could be used to better understand Grian through contemplating how she connects to or is an aspect of Macha.

Invocation to Grian

Queen of the sí of Cnoc Greine
Sister of Áine, daughter of Yew
Lady of the winter solstice
of cold, pale light shining on snow
Grian of the cold winds
Grian of the winter sun
Grian of the fairy hill
I call to you

Danu – Mother of the Gods

Danu is an obscure figure who appears only a handful of times in Irish mythology, and always under the genitive form of the name: "Danann" or "Danand". This has led many to suggest that the name of the Goddess is a reconstruction based on the name

Tuatha Dé Danann, which is often translated as "people of the Goddess Danu". Tuatha Dé Danann itself is problematic as it may be a term added later by the Irish monks to differentiate the native Irish Gods from the biblical characters referred to as "Tuatha Dé" (People of God) in the writings, making the subject slightly more complicated.

Although many people assume Danann only shows up briefly in the Lebor Gabala Erenn, she does also make a couple appearances in the Cath Maige Tuired: *"The women, Badb, Macha, Morrigan and Danann offered to accompany them"* and *"...the three queens, Ere, Fotla and Banba, and the three sorceresses, Badb, Macha and Morrigan, with Bechuille and Danann their two foster-mothers"* (Gray, 1983). It is possible that the second reference is a transcription error and should read "Dinann", which would mean the list included Be Chuille and Dinann, the two daughters of Flidais listed as she-farmers in the Lebor Gabala Erenn, something that would make more sense in the context of the reference. However, the first appearance seems to stand alone. It's also worth noting that genealogies in the mythology are extremely convoluted between sources, so it is also possible based on the way that one redaction of the Lebor Gabala Erenn describes "Danand" as a daughter of Flidais, and later says it is Danu, not Flidais, who is Bechuille's mother, that the reference in the Cath Maige Tuired reflects a different understanding of the Goddesses. Danu is described as "mother of the Gods" and in some versions is equated to Anu, one of the Morrignae and a daughter of Ernmas (Macalister, 1941).

However, in different versions Anu is listed as the seventh daughter of Ernmas, making Danu/Anu a sister to the three Morrignae rather than one of their number. We see her equated to Morrigu and listed as the mother of three sons by her own father as well as mother of all the Gods, for example, here: *"The Morrigu, daughter of Delbaeth, was mother of the other sons of Delbaeth, Brian, Iucharba, and Iuchair: and it is from her additional name 'Danann' the*

Paps of Ana in Luachair are called, as well as the Tuatha De Danann." (Macalister, 1941).

She is sometimes also equated to Brighid because both are listed in different places as the mother of the three sons of Tuireann. It is possible that Danu was a name used for Anu, the Morrigu or Brighid, but is also possible that the later references to Danu were added by monks seeking to give Danu more legitimacy as an important factor among the Gods. The third possibility, of course, is that there were originally regional variations of the stories that placed a different Goddess in the same role depending on which Goddess mattered in what region and the attempt to unify these stories created the muddy waters we have today.

Elsewhere in literature Danu is described as a Goddess and Druidess (O hOgain, 2006). She is sometimes called the mother of the Gods, but in other places is associated specifically with the three Gods of skill (O hOgain, 2006). It is extremely difficult to sort out any coherent list of her possible parentage, siblings, or children. Very little personal information is attributed to her that is not elsewhere applied to someone else, leading me to suspect that at least part of her story was grafted on at a later time.

Many modern authors associate her with the Welsh Don and with continental Celtic Goddesses based on the widespread use of the root word for her name Dánuv, which is associated, for example, with the Danube river. The name Danu itself seems to come from the Proto-Indo-European word for river[6]. She has associations with both rivers and as a Goddess of the earth; she likely was originally a river Goddess whose focus later shifted to the earth (O hOgain, 2006).

In modern myth we can find many new stories that include Danu; these are by nature based on the individual's personal inspiration. Alexei Kondratiev wrote an essay called "Danu and Bile: the primordial parents?" in which he links Danu and Bile as a likely pairing that could represent the parents of the Gods.

Similarly Berresford Ellis also sees Danu and Bile as a pairing. Some modern pagans and Druids have created elaborate creation stories involving these two and internet sources will list Danu as the mother of deities like Cernunnos and the Dagda. It is best to bear in mind the lack of substantial historic evidence relating to this Goddess and take much of the modern myth and information for what it is.

Creating a relationship with this Goddess would be challenging and would rely on personal intuition to a great degree. The lack of substantial information and mythology means we have only hints to work with. She is a river Goddess. She is a land Goddess. She is a mother of many children and a Druidess. Beyond this, let your own inspiration guide you.

The Morrigan in My Life

The Morrigan is a very complex Goddess, as are the other deities that are known under that title. Over the years as I have sought to deepen my knowledge of and connection to the three Morrigans I have also reached out to honor some of these other Goddesses who are so often connected to her. My own experiences have been mixed and I found some genuine connections and others that I did not resonate with at all.

My own personal experiences with Nemain are few. I have encountered her only a handful of times; she appears to me as a naked warrior, painted in the blood of her enemies. Her energy is fierce and terrifying even when she isn't trying to be. I have no personal experience with Fea or Be Neit, as such.

I have honored Aine on midsummer for many years, and am glad I do. My family bakes a cake for her every year, which we give as an offering to her and to the Fair Folk. I'm still not convinced she is one of the Morrigans, but I do think she is a powerful and complex Goddess.

I am only just building an understanding of Grian, but I am comfortable with associating her with the winter solstice and honor her on that day. I feel that she is the hope of growing warmth in winter, and of renewal; the promise of the solstice that the light of each coming day will be longer and that spring, no matter how distant, will arrive. I offer her spiced cider and sugar cookies, and as my family bakes a cake at midsummer for Aine, we dedicate the one we bake at midwinter to Grian.

Danu was actually the very first Irish Goddess I ever honored when I found Irish paganism. I see her in a very broad, all-encompassing way, as the mother of all. She appears to me as an immense woman dressed in green with dark hair and eyes. Her energy is like the earth, immeasurable and solid, and like the ocean, vast and yet with a feeling of movement to it. There is something indescribably old to Danu and an impersonal feeling to her as well.

Chapter Five

The Morrigan in Mythology

The Morrigan appears in a variety of different stories and myths in Ireland. Looking at these appearances and what the Morrigan does in each of them can be enormously helpful in trying to understand who the Morrigan was and is. It is beyond the scope of this work to make an exhaustive study of all of her stories, but I will try to offer the most significant for you to consider. It is also beyond this book to fully retell each story, so the focus will be on the portions featuring the different Morrigans. I strongly encourage people to read the full stories for themselves.

The Morrigan in the Invasion Myths

The Morrigan, Badb, and Macha appear in both the first and second Cath Maige Tuired stories. The first battle of Maige Tuired is the story of the Tuatha Dé Danann coming to Ireland and fighting for the land with the Fir Bólg – primordial beings who were already there. The second battle of Maige Tuired is the tale of the Tuatha Dé Danann fighting against the Fomorians, chthonic beings who they share Ireland with. In both stories the war Goddesses have important roles in defending their people.

In the first battle of Maige Tuired we initially see the three Morrigans when the battle with the Fir Bolg is about to be waged. We are told:

It was then that Badb and Macha and Morrigan went to the Knoll of the Taking of the Hostages, and to the Hill of Summoning of Hosts at Tara, and sent forth magic showers of sorcery and compact clouds of mist and a furious rain of fire, with a downpour of red blood from the air on the warriors' heads; and they allowed the Fir Bolg neither

rest nor stay for three days and nights.
(Fraser, 1915).

The magic of the three sisters is potent and the Fir Bolg are embarrassed that their own magic workers seem so powerless in contrast. Later, during the first round of combat the Fir Bolg poet, seeing the slaughter, declares that: *"The Red Badb will thank them for the battle-combats I look on."* (Fraser, 1915).

When the next battle occurs a list of the nobles of the Tuatha Dé Danann who go to the front to fight is given and with it we are told that Morrigan, Badb, Macha, and Danann accompanied them. Similarly on the fourth day of battle the three Morrigans, as well as their sisters the sovereignty Goddesses Eriu, Fotla, and Banba, and their foster-mothers Danann and Be Chuille, accompany the warriors. In this battle the Goddesses set up pillars behind their own army so that the warriors cannot retreat but must fight. Eventually the Tuatha Dé Danann triumph, although their king Nuada loses his arm during the fighting.

In the second battle of Maige Tuired the Morrigan appears to Lugh to urge him to rise up and fight against the Fomorians who are oppressing the Tuatha Dé Danann. It is this appearance which seems to set in motion the actual war between the two powers.

On Samhain the Morrigan met with the Dagda and they united before she promised to aid the Tuatha Dé Danann in the Cath Maige Tuired. We are told that a year before the battle the Dagda had arranged to meet the Morrigan near Samhain-time. He found her straddling a river, washing, with her hair hanging in nine sections. One foot was on the south shore and one on the north shore. He talked to her and they joined together, after which the site was called "The Bed of the Couple".

After having sex with him, the Morrigan tells the Dagda to gather the skilled Gods together and she will meet them near the river. She promises to go to one of the Fomorian kings, Indech, and to, *"...take from him the blood of his heart and the kidneys of his valor."* (Gray, 1983). When the hosts of the Tuatha Dé Danann meet up with her later she gives them two handfuls of blood as a symbol of her destruction of the king, and that place is called the "Ford of Destruction" afterwards. Although Indech is not killed then, he does die in the following battle, suggesting that her act may have been magical, with the blood representing her taking of his courage and strength, enabling him to be defeated in combat.

When the armies of the Tuatha Dé Danann have gathered and Lugh asks her what she will contribute to the fight she replies: *"'Not hard to say,' ... 'I have stood fast; I shall pursue what was watched; I will be able to kill; I will be able to destroy those who might be subdued.'"* (Gray, 1983). In the battle itself we learn that Macha and Nuada both fall together at the hands of the Fomorian king Balor. Macha is the only female name listed in the recounting of the warriors who died in the battle and because of the context in which her name is given, it is entirely logical to assume she died fighting alongside her husband.

As to the Morrigan herself it was said: *"Then the Morrigu, daughter of Ernmass, came, and heartened the Tuatha De to fight the battle fiercely and fervently. Thereafter the battle became a rout, and the Fomorians were beaten back to the sea."* (Cross & Slover, 1936). After the victory of the Tuatha Dé Danann, Badb is asked to give the news and she recites a prophecy which tells of the fate of the world, both good and bad, to come.

The Morrigan in the Ulster Cycle

The main story of the Ulster cycle is the Táin Bó Cúailgne, the story of a war between two Irish provinces, Connacht and Ulster, over two great bulls who are actually enchanted cowherds that have assumed many shapes over different lifetimes. The primary characters of this Táin are the hero Cu Chulain and the queen of Connacht, Medb, although the story is an epic which covers many years and includes a multitude of other minor characters, including Cu Chulain's charioteer and Medb's husband. The Morrigan also plays a pivotal role as Macha, in a prequel to the main story, Badb, and Morrigu, and we see Nemain and Bé Neit as well.

No relationship in Irish mythology may be more complicated than that of the Morrigan and the epic hero Cu Chulain. Some people feel that their relationship is an antagonistic one, with the Morrigan setting herself against him and ultimately causing his death; others feel that she loved him or otherwise favored him and her actions were designed to increase his glory as a warrior. My own opinion is in the middle – I think that the Morrigan engineered the events of the Táin Bó Cúailgne for her own reasons and she needed Cu Chulain as part of it, but her relationship to him seems largely ambivalent. Her main focus seems to be on the war itself, and she is undeniably its cause. While she clearly favors Ulster, and for that matter the Brown Bull who she had bred to her own cow in the Táin Bó Regamna, she often seems to contend against Cu Chulain and make his path more difficult. At one point in the Táin it is only the intercession of Lugh and his sí warriors who intervene to protect and heal Cu Chulain that prevents his death.

As a prelude to the entire Táin it's important to understand that the events occur because of the curse Macha lays on the men of Ulster, which was previously discussed in the chapter on Macha. This curse lays low the warriors of Ulster when they are in great need, but does not affect Cu Chulain, either because of his youth or because his father is the God Lugh. This means that when the armies of Connacht attack the only one who can defend Ulster is Cu Chulain alone. Had Macha's curse not been on the warriors the entire story would have gone much differently.

Cu Chulain first encounters the Morrigan in the story of the Táin Bó Regamna, after hearing a cow crying out in distress. He searches for the source of the noise and finds a very strange sight: a one-legged horse hitched to a chariot by a pole transfixing its body, with a red-haired, red-cloaked woman in the chariot and a man driving a cow alongside. Cu Chulain tries to speak to the man, challenging their right to the cow, but the woman answers him, responding that it is none of his business. As the encounter goes on with the woman frustrating the hero with her answers, he eventually leaps onto the woman's shoulders, threatening her with his spear. She tells him she is a satirist – a type of poet – and recites a poem for him. He leaps down and throws a spear at her, only to find that all have vanished and the woman has become a raven perched in a nearby tree.

Recognizing her as the Morrigan he says that if he had known it was her from the beginning the encounter would have gone differently, to which she replies that he will suffer for what he has done. He tells her she has no power over him, but she replies that she does indeed and then tells him that she is guarding his death and will continue to do so. She then incites him to battle, telling him that the cow is hers and that she has taken it out of the sí of Cruachan to breed it to the bull of Cualgne, which will lead to the Táin Bó Cúailgne. She also says that he shall die when the cow's unborn calf is a yearling. He welcomes the battle as something that will increase his glory and fame, denying that he will die in the conflict, and she promises to hinder him in three different forms, as an eel tying his feet, as a wolf biting him, and as an Otherworldly cow leading a host of cows against him. To each threat he replies that he shall overcome her and she will not be healed without his blessing. The two part ways and the Morrigan returns to the cave of Cruachan.

The Morrigan initially appears in the Táin Bó Cúailgne itself sitting, either in the form of a woman or crow, on a stone pillar near the Brown Bull, the Donn of Cúailgne, who is pastured with his 50 heifers. She speaks to the bull, warning him of the coming cattle raid so that he moves his herd. This is the second time we know of that she has interacted with the bull, the first being alluded to in the previous Táin Bó Regamna.

We first see Badb when she appears to Queen Medb in a dream and incites her to avenge her son, who has been killed. This is reminiscent of the way that the Morrigan appeared to Lugh in the second battle of Maige Tuired and incited Lugh to fight or the way that she appeared to Cu Chulain in the Táin Bó Regamna and incited him to battle during the future Táin Bó Cúailgne. Inciting warriors to battle is a significant theme for the Morrigan.

When next Cu Chulain and the Morrigan meet she appears to him in the guise of a beautiful young woman, offering him victory if he will sleep with her. He refuses, saying that he has come for battle not for a woman's body. She later appears while he is fighting as a wolf, eel, and heifer, each time causing him to be injured, but is dealt three blows by the hero which he promises he will never agree to heal. She then appears to him as an old woman with a three-teated dairy cow and offers him milk from the cow; after each drink he blesses her, healing one of her wounds. It may seem odd to us that Cu Chulain was so easily lured by a simple offer of milk, but we should remember that the early Irish were a heavily dairy based culture. Early Ireland used a wider range of dairy products than most other contemporary cultures and milk especially was enjoyed in a variety of forms (MacCormick, 2008). The offer of fresh milk to a man in the middle of fighting a war was a great temptation indeed, and I believe the story's audience would have understood why he so easily agreed to drink and blessed the woman offering it to him. After the third blessing, when she was completely healed, she reminded him that he had said he would never offer her his blessing and he replied that if he had known it was her he would not have.

Later in the story Cu Chulain raises a great shout upon seeing the army gathered to fight him, and Nemain appears, shrieking, along with a multitude of dangerous spirits. Her voice is so terrifying that 100 warriors fall dead at hearing it. Gulermovich Epstein suggests that in the Táin Bó Cúailgne Badb often appears around Cu Chulain when he is fighting because of several places where the hero references the great noise she makes around him (Gulermovich Epstein, 1998). Nemain then appears again over the opposing army, this time at night, causing confusion and terror, and in some versions bringing prophetic dreams.

The final time we see the Morrigan in this Táin is when she appears to both armies chanting a poem to incite them to battle. She promises both sides victory, apparently genuinely prophesying it to Ulster, but tricking the other army by encouraging the warriors to a fight they were doomed to lose. It is also possible that her poem was not a prophecy at all but a straightforward incitement to battle, a practice among the early Irish called laíded.

Included in the Ulster Cycle, which the Táin Bó Cúailgne belongs to, is the Aided Conculaind, the Death of Cu Chulain. This story also features the Morrigan in several ways. Before the final battle in which the hero will be killed, the Morrigan appears and breaks his chariot to try to keep him from the fighting, although he seems to perceive it as either a challenge by her or an ill omen. On the morning of the battle his horse, the Grey of Macha, refuses to be harnessed and then cries tears of blood, presaging his death. In some versions of the tale he sees Badb as a washer at the ford as he goes to battle, and knows she is washing his own bloody battle gear, an omen of his death. During the battle itself the Grey of Macha fights fiercely even after being mortally wounded to defend Cu Chulain. When the hero is finally wounded to the point of dying he ties himself to a pillar so that he might remain on his feet and his enemies are so fearful of him that they dare not approach to see if he has died until the story says that: "*And then came the battle Goddess Morrigu and her sisters in the form of scald-crows and sat on his shoulder.*" (Jones, 2014). Only when this happens and they are certain he has died do they come forward to claim their trophy. And with this the Morrigan's promise from the Táin Bó Regamna comes to pass as she did indeed guard his death.

The Morrigan in My Life

My first introduction to the Morrigan did not come in ancient epics, nor in modern paganism. No, my first encounter with her came in a children's book in which she was the villain. The book, by Pat O'Shae, is called *The Hounds of the Morrigan* and to this day it is one of my favorites. It is the story of two children, a brother and sister, who set out on an epic journey into the Otherworld with the help of Angus mac Og and his sister Brighid. They have come into possession of a relic which the Morrigan is also seeking because it is the prison for a powerful creature and if she gets hold of it can give her the power to take over the world. In the story the Morrigan appears as a motorcycle-riding old woman with her two sisters and causes havoc and problems for the two children throughout.

It may seem odd that I like the book so much since it paints the Morrigan as the villain, but as a child I was fascinated by the portrayal of her in the book as well as all the other magical and mystical beings in the story. I was never afraid of this fictional Morrigan or her sisters, but rather I found them fascinating in a way that is hard to describe. I didn't want them to win in the story and yet a part of me sided with them and wanted to see them returned to their former glory, only hinted at in the book. Years later I would pick up the threads of the Morrigan's story in real myth and folklore, but that first introduction, through a child's eyes, has always stayed with me.

Chapter Six

Animals and the Morrigan

The Morrigan and her sisters were strongly associated with several different animals. To better understand the meaning of the forms she takes it is helpful to understand the place each animal held in ancient Irish culture. In the story of the Táin Bó Regamna the Morrigan takes the form of a raven and in the story of Da Derga's Hostel Badb appears as a crow. In the Táin Bó Cúailgne the Morrigan changes into a wolf, eel, and heifer when she is fighting against Cu Chulain. Macha is also associated with crows as well as horses. We will look at each of these animals in turn in the following sections.

Ravens

Called Fiach or Fiach Dubh in Irish, the raven has long been associated with the Morrigan. The raven is one of the forms the Morrigan and Badb are known to take, for example at the end of the Táin Bó Regamna where she transforms into a raven while confronting Cu Chulain. Ravens were seen as symbols of both war – being birds that were drawn to battlefields and fed on carrion – and of prophecy (Green, 1992). Ravens appear on coins and also on armor, and bones from ravens have been found in sacrificial deposit sites among the continental Celts (Green, 1992).

The raven is a well-known bird of omen. Any time ravens are in the area their activity, calls, and direction of flight might be noted and interpreted, often interpreted as an ill omen. If a raven arrives just as a new task is being begun it is seen as an omen that the work will not end well, and a raven near a home signifies a death (O hOgain, 1995). On the other hand, should a raven with white on its wings fly to the right-hand side of a person and call out it was thought to be a sign of great luck for the person

(Anderson, 2008).

Author Glynn Anderson suggests that most Irish lore about the raven is shared by the Norse and reflects Viking influence (Anderson, 2008). In Irish myth ravens are associated with several deities including the Morrigan and Lugh (Anderson, 2008). Ravens are seen as psychopomps who are able to travel between the world of the living and the world of the dead, as well as the Otherworld. They have strong associations as messengers, which may be why they are seen as such powerful birds of omen.

The Hooded Crow

Called Feannóg in Irish, the crow is seen with a similar mix of good and bad omens to ravens. Badb was also called Badb Catha, literally "battle Badb" or "battle crow" and both she and the Morrigan were said to change from human form to crows (Green, 1992). Macha is associated with crows and one meaning of her name is given as Royston crow, an old name for the hooded crow (eDIL, n.d.). When Cu Chulain died a crow, believed to be one of the Morrigans, appeared and perched on his shoulder to signal his death to his enemies (Green, 1992).

Unlike other types of crows, hooded crows are not solid black, but rather the head, chest, wings, and tail are black and everything else is grey. This gives them a distinct appearance that makes them stand out from their all-black cousins. In the Shetland Islands hooded crows are so common that to see black crows was believed to be an omen of starvation to come (Gulermovich Epstein, 1998). As with ravens, a crow landing on the roof of a house or flying over a home was an omen of death or disaster, but others believe that bad luck comes when crows leave an area (O hOgain, 1995; Anderson, 2008). It was believed that witches, fairies, bansidhe, and Badb appeared as hooded crows in Ireland, a belief that was especially strong in County Clare, and they were thus seen as unlucky (Anderson, 2008).

Generally crows and ravens seem to be treated almost inter-
changeably in stories.

Wolves

Wolves were significant animals to the Celts long before they
came to Ireland, and doubtless played a role for the native
Neolithic peoples as well. From archaeological sources we know
that the continental Celts hunted wolves for their fur and to use
their bones and teeth for jewelry (Green, 1992). In later periods
wolves were popular images in artwork as well, appearing alone
or paired with deer (Green, 1992). The battle horn, or carnyx,
which was blown in battle to create a loud fearsome noise, was
sometimes made in the shape of a wolf's head, and warriors'
armor was sometimes decorated with images of wolves (Green,
1992). Warriors were also sometimes called wolfsheads, or
coinchenn, in Irish (eDIL, n.d.).

Several different sources talk about Celtic tribes that believed
they were descended from wolves (Monaghan, 2004). Wolves
were also associated with the night-time and the underworld, as
well as being an animal connected symbolically with warriors
due to its fierceness (Green, 1992; MaCulloch, 1911). Taking all of
this information together we can perhaps come to associate
wolves with the dead and with the wilderness as well as battle,
all things which can easily be related to the Morrigan as well.

Wolves also had a strong association with outlaws and with
shapeshifting. The word folc means both wolf and lawless
brigand (eDIL, n.d.). In myth there was sometimes an assumption
that outlaws could take the form of wolves and in some cases that
a person's spirit could fare forth in the form of a wolf (Koch,
2005).

Dogs were the domesticated face of the wolf and it is interesting to note that one of the forms used by the Morrigan when
she came at Cu Chulain, whose name means "the hound of
Culan", was that of a wolf. At the time Cu Chulain was defending

Ulster and might be seen to represent right order and honorable behavior, so the Morrigan coming at him in a form associated with outlawry and being outside the bounds of society creates an interesting layer of symbolism to the event.

Eels and Snakes

The Morrigan takes the form of an eel when fighting against Cu Chulain and it is said that her son Meche has three serpents or snakes in his heart which could have destroyed Ireland. Eels are a native species in Ireland, but snakes are not found there, having been extinct since the last Ice Age. Eels therefore have a definite real world quality to them, while snakes have a clearly mythic quality to them. Miranda Green in her book *Animals in Celtic Life and Myth* suggests that snakes symbolize death, destruction, evil, healing, fertility, and are connected to water (Green, 1992). Interestingly many Irish stories featuring "snakes" involve water snakes, or snakes living in water, suggesting that Green's association of the two, snakes and water, may have some merit in Irish symbolism.

It is difficult to say why the Morrigan appeared to Cu Chulain not as a supernatural snake (remember there were no snakes in Ireland so any references to such are clearly discussing a supernatural or Otherworldly element) but as a very natural eel, except that the story may have been emphasizing that she approached him in three forms that represented natural animals. Additionally Badb is connected to the concepts of serpents and venom, and Nemain's name may mean venomous (Gulermovich Epstein, 1998).

Cows

The cow, bó in Irish, and bull, or tarbh, were significant in many Irish stories because Irish society was based on cattle owning; wealth was measured in cattle and cattle raids were significant events and formed their own branch of literature, called tána.

The cow was the backbone of a person's social standing, the basic monetary unit, and was used to settle legal disputes as the means to pay fines (MacCormick, 2008). Within this it is important to realize that certain types of animals had greater values than others, with a milk cow ranking highest (MacCormick, 2008).

Many Irish Goddesses were associated with cows, either appearing in the form of cows, owning magical cows, having cows who gave huge amounts of milk or being reared on milk from a magical cow. When we first see the Morrigan in the form of a cow in the Táin Bó Cúailgne she is described as a hornless red heifer; a heifer is a young cow that has not yet born a calf and would be of less value. Later in the same story she appears as an old woman with a milk cow and uses the produce of the animal to trick Cu Chulain into healing her after he swore he wouldn't. Cu Chulain's first meeting with the Morrigan also involved a cow, as he tried to stop her from driving a cow he believed she had stolen and which would eventually set off the events of the famous Táin Bó Cúailgne.

Cattle appear in artwork, symbolizing prosperity and reflecting the herding culture of the Celts (Green, 1992). It is also possible that the design of ringforts was influenced by cattle, as evidence suggests that the structures were used to protect cattle from raiding, or at least that cattle were kept within them (MacCormick, 2008). In a modern context it can be difficult for us to understand exactly how important, how pivotal, cows were in early Irish society. They were money, they were social standing, they were the source of a main food product, they were art motifs and a factor in designing forts. For the Morrigan to appear as a cow and in relation to cows, especially cattle raids, carries a profound significance that it's important for us to at least try to understand.

The Morrigan is associated with cows in several ways. As we have seen she takes the form of a cow and appears with a cow in the Táin Bó Cúailgne. She also steals cows in several stories including the Echtra Nerai and Odras. In the story of Odras the Morrigan steals a bull which a woman named Odras tries to get back. The woman pursues the bull back to the cave of Cruachan but then falls asleep. Finding her this way the Morrigan turns Odras into a river. While her motives in the tale of Odras are hard to understand; usually when she is stealing cows the larger purpose relates to starting cattle raids – effectively starting wars.

Horses

Horses have long been seen as sacred animals in Irish paganism. Evidence shows the presence of horses in Ireland as far back as 3000 BCE and we know that during the Celtic period they played an important role (O hOgain, 2006). Horses were a status symbol, a very practical means of transportation, work animals, and also served in warfare, the Irish fighting mounted and with chariots. Many Irish Gods are associated with horses, including Macha, Aine, Dagda, and Manannan (O hOgain, 2006). Aine, for example, was said to take the form of a red mare and travel around the area near Knockainey. Horses often figure in mytho-logical tales; for example Cu Chulain's horses played a role in the Táin Bó Cuailgne, with one of them, the Grey of Macha, weeping prophetic tears of blood before the hero's death. The horses of Donn are said to escort the dead to the Otherworld, by some accounts, and horses were believed to be able to see ghosts and spirits (O hOgain, 2006). Horse skulls and long bones, like human ones, were preserved in ossuaries and there have been archeological finds that included the ritual burial of horses that are believed to have died naturally, showing the importance that the Celts gave to horses (Green, 1992).

Even up until more modern times horse symbolism was important, and we see things like the Lair Bhan (white mare) – a person dressed up in a white sheet holding a carved horse head or skull who led a procession from house to house at Samhain. Holidays like Lughnasa prominently featured horse racing, which might be a race over a flat course or involve the riders swimming the horses across a river. A very old Irish belief was that horses had once been able to speak as humans could and that they were still able to understand people, making it important to always speak kindly to them (O hOgain, 2006).

There are also a wide array of beliefs relating to Otherworldly horses like the Each Uisce and Kelpie; the movie Into the West deals with the story of an Otherworldly horse's relationship with two children in modern Ireland. It was believed that the seventh filly in a row born of the same mare (with no colts in between) was a lucky and blessed animal, called a fiorlair, a true mare (O hOgain, 2006). A true mare was naturally exempt from witchcraft and fairy enchantments, and this protection extended to her rider (Monaghan, 2004). Horses in general were lucky and would be walked over newly plowed fields, in the belief that a horse trampling freshly planted seed would make the crops grow better (O hOgain, 2006). Many protective charms and superstitions are aimed at protecting horses from the evil eye, fairy mischief and general ill health.

At least one author suggests that eating horse meat was taboo in Ireland except under rare ritual circumstances; although we know that horses were eaten in Gaul and southern England they did not seem to be considered a food animal in Ireland (Monaghan, 2004; Green, 1992). Reflecting the sacred and important place that horses had in the culture, sites in Gaul that include the remains of sacrificed horses usually also include human sacrificial remains (Green, 1992). We have one anecdotal report of horses being sacrificed and eaten in Ireland, in association with the crowning of a king. A ritual was enacted in Ulster, according to Gerald Cambrensis writing in the 13th century, where the new king had sex with a white mare who was then killed and stewed; the king bathed in the stew and then ate it, as did the gathered people (Puuhvel, 1981). This ritual is assumed to have ties to the horse's symbolism and represented the king joining with the Goddess of sovereignty. This report though is problematic in several ways. It occurred very late into the Christian period, well after the conversion of the country, and the author makes his disdain for the Irish abundantly clear in his book *Topographia Hibernica*, where he says the Irish people are savage and lack any civilization. This makes his story about a barbaric king-making rite with bestiality and sacrificial feasting hard to trust on face value (Wright, 1913).

A Note on Animal Sacrifice and Sacred Animals

Ritual animal sacrifice is a complicated subject in its own right. It is up to the reader to decide whether the practice is allowable within their own spiritual framework. However, it would be wise to respect the practices of others even when they differ from our own. Many people are categorically against the practice, but many others see it as integral to what they do in their attempts to reconstruct or honor the historic faith. I am not going to try to change anyone's opinion on animal sacrifice in general, but I would like to encourage everyone to consider the appropriateness of the choice of animals when it is done.

Although I support traditional religious animal sacrifice in a Celtic context I am absolutely against sacrificing or eating horses. This is a controversial topic, but my opinion on this is firm. At one time I had held a different view on this, which was born, I must admit, out of a hesitance to judge modern cultures that still eat horses. But the reality is I can judge the practice as wrong – like eating whale, dog, or tiger, which I am also against – without condemning the entire culture that does it.

The ritual recorded by Gerald is a main one used by modern people wanting to do horse sacrifices to defend the idea. However, it should be obvious for several reasons why this ritual does not justify modern horse sacrifice. Firstly, it was rarely done, if we credit Gerald's account, and only on the most significant of events, the crowning of a king and his marriage to the land. We have no modern equivalent to this. Secondly the ritual also involved public bestiality and bathing in the food before it was served; I hope the reasons not to do this are self-evident. Beyond this, as can be seen by the Gaulish examples of interred horse and human sacrifices, the ritual killing of horses seems to have been viewed as an occasion of the utmost gravity, on par with offering a human life. Green theorizes that these events related to the fulfillment of battle pledges, where a warrior going to fight promised to give to the Gods all the spoils of war, including weapons, horses, and human captives in exchange for victory (Green, 1992).

Just as we no longer practice human sacrifice because it goes against our social norms and morality, so too should we leave horse sacrifice in the past. Horses, like dogs, are animals that we have domesticated to work with us and as pets; they are not food. In the past our ancestors may – or may not – have eaten them, but they also had far fewer options than we do; they needed to eat their domestic pets – we don't. It's also important to realize that most domestic animals, especially horses, that are later used for food but are not raised as food animals, are exposed to a variety of chemicals, including painkillers like Phenylbutazone, that are extremely dangerous for humans to consume.

I also feel strongly that it is wrong to sacrifice horses to Macha especially. In Irish myth it is almost always geis (a ritual taboo or prohibition) to eat the animal that represents or is connected to you; Cu Chulain has a geis against eating dog, Dairmud has a geis not to hunt the boar that is magically bound to him, and Conaire cannot hunt birds, to give some examples. Since horses are Macha's animal it follows that killing or eating them would be offensive to her so they would not be an animal offered to her. I personally received a geis against eating horse when I became her priestess so I admit to having some bias on the subject but I feel the argument against it is strong. As MucCulloch says in *The Religion of the Ancient Celts*, "*Fatal results following upon the killing or eating of an animal with which the eater was connected by name or descent are found in the Irish sagas."* (Macculloch, 1911).

Logic would tell us that if it is geis to eat or harm an animal connected to a person in this way then it would hold true that it would also be taboo to sacrifice certain animals to Gods they were strongly associated with. There is also evidence from other Celtic areas that certain animals were not killed or eaten due to their sacred nature or association with specific deities (MacCulloch, 1911). We do not have a single concrete example from myth or folklore of horses being sacrificed to Macha and we do have evidence that killing or eating a symbolic animal was taboo. It is also worth considering that this would hold true for the other Morrigans and their sacred animals as well.

The Morrigan in My Life

Animals can often appear as omens, and the animals of the Morrigan, especially crows and ravens, are seen by many as her messengers, appearing in portentous ways. The important thing with her animals is not only to respect and honor them but also to be aware of them. Not everything is an omen of course, sometimes an eel is just an eel, after all, but if we remain aware of what is going on around us we can catch glimpses of the numinous.

In June of 2014 I was privileged to attend a retreat dedicated to the Morrigan that lasted for three days. The retreat took place at Temenos in Massachusetts, an off-the-grid retreat center. It was an amazing and transformative experience that included rituals to Badb, Macha, and Anu, as well as workshops, music, and fellowship with people who honor the Morrigan from a wide array of pagan traditions and belief systems. We had all come together, some from very far away both in miles and points of view, for that single purpose, and the weekend was a beautiful example of what we can do as a community when we set aside our differences for a common goal.

The entire time I was there I did not see a single crow. I did not hear them calling. I noticed this absence keenly because crows are very common where I live and I am used to seeing and hearing them throughout the day. I had not even realized how used to it I was until I was in a place where they weren't. After the weekend was over, as we were driving away down and off the mountain we reached a section of road where dirt became pavement, where we transitioned from the sacred space of the retreat to the mundane reality of daily life. As we passed this line three crows flew from right to left across our path and I knew, with absolute certainty, that it was an omen and also a blessing.

Chapter Seven

Finding the Morrigan in the Modern World

The Morrigan in the modern world is at least as complicated as the historical Goddess. Many people today have been called by her and each one will have different views and opinions. In all honesty an entire book could be written just surveying these modern beliefs and still fail to encompass the fullness of her modern interpretations. To some people she is still the historic Goddess, but exists now in a modern context and adapted to the modern world; to others the Morrigan they know bears little resemblance to the ancient Irish Goddess of battle and death.

I do not believe I can tell you how to relate to her or how she might come to you because while she certainly has her own personality that makes her herself and distinct from others, she can also choose how she interacts with each of us. At the end of each previous chapter I have tried to share bits and pieces of my own feelings and experiences with her and with them to show what a modern relationship can be like. In this chapter I would like to present some further food for thought about relating to the Morrigan in the modern world.

Redefining "Dark" Gods

One of the most pervasive modern views of the Morrigan is that she is a Dark Goddess. Since I have been pagan I have regularly run across the concept of Dark Gods, usually deities of war, battle, death, or the underworld. The term dark in this case indicates an association between the deity and the aspects of life or the world that people tend to fear; Gods like Kali, Baba Yaga, Odin, Ares, Hecate, and of course the Morrigan are often referred to as being Dark Gods. Some people will advise avoiding such deities altogether while others will say that approaching them requires extra caution and care. They are said to be less forgiving than other Gods, generally, and harsher. Dark Goddesses often fill the role of Crone in traditions that follow Graves' Maiden-Mother-Crone division of the divine feminine, and Dark Gods are often said to rule over the dark half of the year, further associating them with things that many people perceive as frightening or negative. These ideas can be found in books, websites, and online conversations easily and have become commonplace beliefs in neopaganism. I certainly have fallen into this general line of thinking as a sort of default, even though I am dedicated to deities that are usually described as dark and am a polytheist who follows a different cosmology than mainstream neopaganism.

What I have come to realize is that the entire idea of Dark Gods is, in many ways, an illusion. It is based in a focus on the deities associated with things that we, as modern people, fear because we usually are disconnected from them. Most modern people, especially those with no direct experience of battle and war, look at these concepts as negatives to be avoided, and see the Gods associated with them in a similar light, whereas to our ancestors Gods of battle and war had an important place. Death is feared, especially in our culture where death is often portrayed as an enemy to be fought and most of us are removed from the reality of death since we don't even raise and kill our own food, never mind deal with the hands-on reality of people dying. Even the underworld of the Dark Gods – home of the dead – is seen by some as a place to be avoided because to consider the underworld as a good thing is, on some level, to accept the inevitable death of the self. We fear what these Gods represent and so we fear them.

This view is also rooted in dualism, an approach to deity that would have been foreign to our ancestors (well most of them anyway). It plays into that dreaded either/or mindset that sees everything opposed to something else. To believe in Dark Gods is to, logically, believe in Light Gods, for if the Dark Gods are the ones connected to what we fear then the remaining Gods must be connected to that which we do not fear. When I think about it in these terms I find it very problematic. The contrast between one group and the other seems to be a reflection of nothing more profound than a modern divine popularity contest, or a reflection of the historic filtering process where the pagan Gods were viewed through a foreign lens and categorized from that perspective.

People say that Dark Gods are harsh when crossed or offended – are the other Gods less so? Doesn't mythology show us that any deity when offended is likely to react badly? People say that Dark Gods are the teachers of hard lessons – but are the other Gods' lessons any easier? Or isn't it just that we can feel more comfortable with a Goddess of healing than a Goddess of battle, even though both deserve equal respect?

It is true that the Gods usually called dark are known for some of their negative interactions with people, yet there are also examples of positive interactions. In the same way the non-dark deities are usually seen as gentle or safe, yet we can often find examples of them acting against our interests or punishing those who offend them. Áine is seen as a Goddess of the sun and fertility by some and yet she is also the consort of Crom Cruach who seeks to steal the harvest each year. The Dagda is a God of wisdom and abundance, yet he possesses a club that can strike eight men dead at one blow. My point here is that the Gods are all complex beings that can never be defined in such broad strokes or absolutes.

There is also the risk with this view of missing important nuances of a deity by focusing exclusively on one narrow aspect of what that God relates to. The Morrigan is not only a Goddess of war. To focus only on her role as a war Goddess is to lose the depth and breadth of her power and personality. Every deity labeled dark is more complex and diverse than any simple label can convey. To approach them otherwise is to reduce the deity to a caricature.

I am devoted to several deities often defined as dark, and yet I do not approach them this way – they are simply the Gods who called to me and who bless my life. Really how can I call dark, with all the implications of that term, powers who have supported my life and responded to my prayers? How could I ever urge people not to honor my Gods, or even to fear them, when they have done so much good for me? Certainly they deserve to be approached with respect, but that is no more or less true for the Morrigan than it is for Brighid. And when we put so much emphasis on treating one group of Gods with such fear and caution isn't there the danger of becoming lax with the others and treating them with less?

In the future I am not going to divide the Gods this way. I will give all the ones I honor equal respect and treat them with equal caution, and be aware of the tendency to become too comfortable with the "Light" Gods and too fearful of the "Dark" Gods. Because I see now that each individual deity has both dark and light, both positive and negative, within them.

For people just coming to the Morrigan I urge you to think about what the term Dark Goddess means to you. For those who are afraid of her war and battle connections, think about why she brings those feelings out in you. For those who only see her as death and blood, why are you avoiding her other associations? For those who only acknowledge her other qualities and reject her harsh features altogether, ask yourself why you fear her strength. Looking at what she makes us feel and trying to understand why we feel that way can be enormously helpful in creating a stronger connection to her.

"Working With" the Morrigan

There is a common expression in neopaganism, where a person will say that they "work with" certain deities; generally what they actually mean is either that they worship those deities, or that they call on them for a specific purpose. In my experience among Reconstructionists it is considered disrespectful to say you work with a deity, because however you view the Gods they are not usually seen as our partners in projects. Patrons, perhaps, or guides, but not partners as another person would be to work with us. It's an interesting bit of semantics between the two approaches to paganism. In neopaganism the phrase is used commonly and doesn't seem to even register with most people, while in Reconstructionist faiths you don't tend to see it used and when it is it can become the focus of the discussion as people debate the accuracy or blasphemy of it. Many neopagans tend to see the entire concept and nature of deity in a way that lends itself to the idea of Gods helping us for no reason except that we ask for the help, while recons tend to see our relationship to deity as based on reciprocity and balance.

I believe that to work with a deity is closer to the client/patron type relationship that is seen in Reconstructionist approaches, where very specific guidelines and goals are needed, and offerings are made, as well as divination to ascertain that the deity involved is willing and agreeable. It goes beyond the patron/client relationship though, in my opinion, because it is more invasive and intense – and I highly recommend setting a very clear time limit. The value is that connecting to, trusting, and allowing a deity to help you on that level is more profound than anything else can be, I believe, and can accomplish things that might otherwise not be achieved. If, of course, you are willing to pay the price of doing it.

In my experience many people initially coming to the Morrigan do so with the idea of working with her in the neopagan context. This is not always the case of course as some people do choose to worship her without the overtones of working with her, but I have found it to be common. In some cases it's not the person reaching out to her, but rather the

Morrigan who makes her presence known to them. Sometimes she comes to a person for a specific purpose and other times she comes and stays, whatever our intentions were going into it. It's always best to remember that once you invite a deity in – in any context – you can never be entirely sure how the relationship will go. It also happens sometimes that a person invites her in but she does not respond to them.

There are many reasons why someone might want to temporarily honor or work with the Morrigan. It is a very old belief that if a God could give something they could also take it away, so the Morrigan who brings terror, battle frenzy/rage, and madness could be prayed to – or worked with – if a person wants relief from those issues. As a Goddess of sovereignty, especially as Macha, she can also be worked with to gain a better sense of self and of self-empowerment. As a Goddess of prophecy she can help a person gain skill in that area as well. If you choose to work with her, rather than worship her, I suggest setting a time limit and strict guidelines. Agree up front to what you're willing to pay, and know that she always collects.

Modern Altars

One of the first steps in creating a connection to any deity is creating an altar space for them. The altar is a focal point of worship, a place to leave offerings, a place to pray, and a place to go to feel connected. Sometimes an altar will be permanent, other times temporary, but in any case it serves as an important way for us to create a tangible space to commune with our Gods.

Exactly what is on a modern altar and how the altar is used can vary widely and generally each tradition or faith will have guidelines or expectations for the set-up of an altar. Most altars that I have seen will include sacred images, candles, and a place or bowl for offerings, but some may also include a variety of objects and tools. My own altars tend to get very elaborate as I try to include a variety of things that are important to me, but I have seen some that are as simple as a candle and incense burner. Creating an altar for the Morrigan, whether for Anu or one of the other Morrigans, is a very personal thing to do. It should reflect your own understanding of the deity the altar is meant to honor, but basic suggestions would include imagery related to the Goddess or things symbolic of her. For Anu this might include statues of the different animal forms she assumes, while Macha might include horses and crows, and Badb might include crows and ravens. Statues of the Morrigan can also be included and there are several very good ones to be found out there including ones by Dryad Designs and Sacred Source. You can also consider making your own with clay or using pictures or artwork. Beyond that many people include things like swords, spears, or knives, representations of rivers or hills, and sometimes cauldrons. Your altar is your place to connect and worship so it should be set up in a way that speaks to you and works for you.

Prayers, Meditation, and Offerings to the Morrigan

Another way to create or strengthen a relationship with the Morrigan is through regular practices including prayers, meditation, and offerings. I have found it very important for myself to have a regular practice that includes these things and I truly believe that such practices will benefit anyone of any spirituality. They allow us to interact with the Gods we honor in active ways; prayer is speaking to the Gods, meditation is listening to the Gods, and offerings are a way to express tangible gratitude for the blessings in our lives.

I have included a variety of prayers in earlier chapters that you can use, or you can make up your own. I find that people often hesitate to make up their own prayers, but don't be afraid to try. Speaking from your heart and being genuine has more value than the most beautiful prayers recited by rote without any heart. If you are really uncertain you can follow a general guideline of naming who you are praying to, stating something about them, and stating why you are praying to them. For example:

Morrigan, Battle Goddess
Mother of fierce warriors
Inciter of cattle-raids
May I find my fierceness
May my passion be incited
Morrigan, inspire my strength
Let it be so

Meditation can take a variety of forms, from simply calming your mind and being open to messages, to guided meditations[7], to more involved spiritual journeywork. The most important thing with this is that you do it regularly and allow yourself to be open to listening. My daily meditation practice often consists of walking meditation where I walk and clear my mind and simply listen. It really doesn't have to be more elaborate than that every day, although more rigid types of meditation are also good. The idea is simply to open ourselves up to hear the Gods when they speak, just as prayer is talking to them while they (hopefully!) listen.

Here is an example of a very basic guided meditation to meet the Morrigan:

Sit comfortably where you won't be disturbed. Take several slow, deep breathes. Close your eyes. See yourself walking down a sunlit path through the woods. The trees are heavy around you, the sun filtering in through the leaves. As you walk the trees slowly begin to thin. You realize there is a clearing ahead and you move towards it. The trees open up and you step into an open space, surrounded by a circle of trees. The air is still and silent, as if the world was holding its breath. Into the stillness steps a figure – it is one of the Morrigans. Look at the figure – how does she appear to you? Stepping towards you she tells you her name and gives you a message. Take as long as you need, and when the Morrigan leaves turn and go back down the path. Go back through the tunnel of trees. The trees around you begin to grow denser, thicker as you walk. The light gets darker. Take several deep breathes. Feel yourself fully back in your body. Wiggle your fingers and toes, stretch. Open your eyes when you are ready.

Offerings are a big part of recon faiths but something that can be underemphasized or ignored in some other branches of paganism. I truly believe though that people of all spiritualities can benefit from this practice. An offering is anything given in a sacred way to the Gods or spirits, and this can include physical items like food, incense, or jewelry, or non-physical items like song, poetry and energy. The Morrigan has also been known to take offerings of blood from the person, or offerings of swords and silver. Intent is very important here; offerings should never just be thrown down or hurriedly given but should always be treated in a sacred way. You can say something aloud when you make an offering, such as a prayer, or you can silently focus on what you are doing. Treat the offering as a holy act: take your time, be reverential, be focused, and whether the offering is a small thing or a huge thing give it from your heart.

Generally if you make offerings you should have either an offering bowl on your altar to place them in or a special place outdoors to leave them. If its outdoors, make sure the place will not be disturbed by other people and that what you leave won't harm the animals or plants in the area. Tangible offerings can be buried or burned; it was an old Irish and wider Celtic practice that an item being offered would be ritually "killed" in this world by bending or breaking it so that it could never be used again by a human. This was a way to give it fully to the Gods and is something we can still do today.

Seasonal Celebrations

Another great way to create a connection to the Morrigan, beyond some of the daily or regular practices, is celebrating seasonal rites in her honor. Obviously you could choose to honor her at any holiday, but she does tend to have associations with certain ones that make those days more appropriate. You can use your imagination in deciding how to incorporate her into your personal celebrations, but these are some ways she relates to different holidays:

- Bealtaine was the day when the Gods arrived in Ireland, and in some versions it was during this time that the three Morrigans used magic against the Fomorians. It is a good time to celebrate the Morrigans as witches, sorceresses, or Druids.
- Midsummer was the date when the Gods fought the Fir Bolg. In the Cath Maige Tuired, during this battle Badb is mentioned, so it might be appropriate to honor Badb now.
- Lughnasa is associated with Macha; fairs were held during this time at her ritual center of Emain Macha. It is a good time to honor Macha as a Goddess of sovereignty and the land.
- Samhain is associated with the second battle of Maige Tuired and it was around this time that the Morrigan joined with the Dagda. It would be appropriate to retell this story and to honor Morrigan as Queen of the Dead or Badb in her role as prophetess.
- Midwinter can possibly be associated with Grian, who may be associated with Macha.

Reconstructing Celtic Seership with Badb

I consider seership a significant part of my practice because I see the taking of omens as essential in ritual. I also keep in mind the Irish triad which says: "Three signs of wisdom: patience, closeness, the gift of prophecy." (Meyers, 1906). In my book *Where the Hawthorn Grows* I discuss my approach to Irish seership practices, but I don't talk about what I actual do, so here I thought I'd talk about my reconstruction and practice of three methods of Irish seership and how they relate to my honoring of the Morrigan.

There were three specific seership practices written about in Ireland and these were imbas forosna – "manifesting knowledge", tenm laida – "illumination of song", and dichetal do chennaib – "extemporaneous poetry" (Matthews, J., 1999). Each of these methods is somewhat obscure and requires both research and inspiration to make usable in a modern context. I firmly believe though that it is possible to reconstruct these methods in effective ways.

Imbas forosnai involves preparing and eating meat (pig, cat, or dog historically or pig today), making an offering to the Gods with specific chants and then lying down with the hands covering the eyes and sleeping or meditating for up to three days undisturbed to receive knowledge or an answer. Another well-known version of this may be the tarbh feis, which involves the sacrifice of a bull, eating its flesh and then wrapping up in its hide for the same purpose. The practice of retreating into a dark room, wrapped in a cloak to receive inspiration – possibly a later version of imbas forosnai, I think – was seen in the Scottish Highlands until a few hundred years ago (Bell, 1703).

For the purposes of modern practice I use two versions of this method. The first is closer to the later Scottish version; I lie down in a darkened room, beneath a cloak, cover my eyes and enter a meditative trance state while focusing on the question I am trying to answer. The second is closer to the older descriptions of imbas forosnai and takes more time and preparation, beginning with cooking a pork roast. In the original ritual the meat was eaten raw, but for modern purposes and safety reasons I cook mine. Some of the pork is ritually offered to Badb[8], who I call on for prophecy, and some is eaten by me. I have special prayers I say to her. After eating the meat I go somewhere quiet, and pray:

Badb, who sees what has not yet come to pass
Who spoke the great prophecy when the battle
Between the Tuatha De and the Fomorians ended
Who spoke of both great peace and an end to all
Help me now to see what I need to see
To find the answer to the question I have
Open the way for me to receive my answer

I lay down in a comfortable position and cover my eyes with my hands. To enter into a trance state I repeatedly chant to myself:

Badb Goddess of prophecy
May I see the past and the future
May I know the Truth of what is
May I find what I seek, and speak it
Badb, open the way for me
To see, to know, to speak
To prophecy of what was and
What is, and what will be
Badb, Goddess of prophecy
May it be so

After repeating this over and over I eventually fall into a trance where I receive the answer. Sometimes it may come as words or a direct message, other times as images.

Tenm laida seems to be, based on its appearance in myths, a type of light trance that a person could enter to answer specific questions, sometimes associated with touching the object directly and other times with putting the tips of the fingers or thumb in the mouth, such as in the stories of Finn mac Cool. In some stories it appears as a method to read the past or identify a body, although this also appears to be a type of seership practiced by both Scathach and Fidelm in mythology when answering questions about the future (Matthews, J., 1999). This method reminds me strongly of psychometry and my own version is very similar to that modern practice. Both imbas forosnai and tenm laida were outlawed by the Christian Church for calling on "idols", so when I use tenm laida I begin with a short chant to the Gods and spirits based on my version of an augury charm:

Gods over me, Gods under me,
Gods before me, Gods behind me,
Knowledge of truth, not knowledge of falsehood,
That I shall truly see all I search for.
Kindly spirits and Gods of life,
May you give me eyes to see all I seek,
May I see and speak truly

Then I either touch the object or put my hands to my mouth and open myself to what comes. This method, naturally, takes a great deal of practice, but it's actually a fun one to use that can be done just for practice, as opposed to the other two methods, which require either more ritual or a higher degree of trance and aren't used as lightly. The real trick with tenm laida is learning to open yourself to the impressions and information that comes when you ask and get accurate results; the tendency can be to fall into imagination or to be so self-critical that you can't relax enough to receive anything.

The third method is dichetal do chenaib, which seems to resemble tenm laida but involve a deeper trance and the spontaneous speaking of poetry to answer the question. Perhaps the Prophecy of the Morrigan could be viewed as this type of method. Dichetal do chenaib was not outlawed as it didn't directly call on pagan deities or spirits and was seen as a part of the poet's art. Dichetal do chenaib requires spontaneous recitation of poetry, which by itself is both a challenge and an art form. When I use this method I go into a trance and wait to see what answer comes to the question, and then do my best to channel that answer into a coherent poetic response. I like to use a form where the last word in one "line" is the first word in the next, creating an internal rhythm to the response. I admit though that I find this method the hardest of the three to actually use and so tend to use it the least.

The Morrigan in My Life

My first direct experience with the Morrigan occurred in the context of working with her, when I went to her/them and asked for help in overcoming certain fears and past traumas that I felt were holding me back. I knew that it was an old belief that those deities who could bring or cause a thing could also cure that thing, which is why I chose the three Morrigans to go to in order to deal with those negative feelings that they were so strongly associated with. I did it out of sheer naivety and with no idea of the profound repercussions that would unfold, but in the long run I am glad that I did it. I say during that time I worked with her, but perhaps it's more accurate to say that they worked with me – like clay being worked by a sculptor.

Unlike the more well-known patron dynamic this involved a great deal of direct influence, that might be called hands-on, and is not similar to any other type of relation to deity I have ever had, from casual worship to out-right dedication. The cost of the experience was high, but I believe the result was far more than I ever could have accomplished on my own, so I do think that this type of work has value, if its entered into with the right mindset and understanding of the consequences. Of course knowing better now I advise caution before jumping into that sort of thing. In my case I spent six months with my entire life in chaos and was made to confront some of my greatest fears, in reality, in a way that re-shaped who I was as a person on more than one level, and effected changes that are still lasting more than 15 years later. I am a different person now than I was then, because of that "work".

Conclusion

The Morrigan, in many guises, is active in the world today. She is seeking people – not only warriors, but many different kinds of people – to honor her, to speak her name again, to bring her worship into the modern world. She is a powerful presence just as she always has been.

Looking at the historic evidence we can see that the Morrigan is a Goddess who appears in many stories as an instigator of war and inciter of battle. She causes conflict and urges warriors on, as well as predicting the outcomes of battles. In some cases she also interferes directly in those outcomes, appearing and offering victory to one side if they will pay her price, or in other cases working to aid the side she favors to ensure their victory. She is a Goddess of strategy who plans far in advance and maneuvers things to create situations and results which she wants. She is associated with many animals, but perhaps none more strongly than cattle and crows, which feature prominently in many of her stories. She is ultimately a Goddess of war, but war as the ancient Irish understood it, *"...in her various forms she embodies... crech: glory and horror, the carnage, the noble beauty, the plundering, the sense of fatal destiny, the noise, the fury."* (Gulermovich Epstein, 1998).

Alongside the Morrigan we have her sisters Macha and Badb who are complexes Goddesses in their own right and also bear the title of Morrigan. Where the Morrigan is associated most strongly with cattle, Macha is connected equally strongly to horses and Badb to crows; all three together share a connection to crows and ravens. Macha is a Goddess of sovereignty, battle, and the land while Badb is a Goddess or battle, prophecy, and terror. All three of the Morrigans are war and death deities and when they appear together it is most often in contexts relating to those subjects.

Besides the three Morrigans there are several other Goddesses who often share the title of Morrigan or are mentioned in relation to it. Each of these may or may not actually be one of the Morrigans, but understanding who they are and why they are connected to that title is important to better understanding who and what the Morrigan is. It is no simple thing to look at the complex web of relations between the different Irish Goddesses in mythology and try to conceptualize how each relates to the other and, more importantly, how certain names which are also titles might apply in different ways. In the same way we can look at the different animal forms that the Morrigans take and the symbolic value of those animals in order to gain a better understanding of the depth of these complex Goddesses.

Connecting to the Morrigan is a lifelong process. Learning about her history and her place in mythology is one step. Reading about another person's experiences with her is another step, as is creating an altar or shrine to her and praying to her regularly. But the next step is to experience her for yourself. If you hear her call, take what you have learned here and let yourself create that connection. Be bold. Be brave. Be her raven.

Bibliography

Anderson, G., (2008) *Birds of Ireland: Facts, Folklore & History*

Banshenchus (n.d.) *Book of Leinster*. Retrieved from http://www
.maryjones.us/ctexts/banshenchus.html

Bell, M., (1703) *A Description of the Western Isles of Scotland*

Berresford Ellis, P., (1987) *A Dictionary of Irish Mythology*

Bonevisuto, N., (2014) *By Blood, Bone, and Blade: A Tribute to the Morrigan*

Chadwick N., (1935) *Imbas Forosnai*. Retrieved from http://searchingforimbas.blogspot.com/p/imbas-forosnai-by-nora-k-chadwick.html

Clark, R., (1990) *The Great Queens: Irish Goddesses from the Morrigan to Cathleen Ni Houlihan*

Coe, E., (1995) *Macha and Conall Cernach: A Study of Two Iconographic Patterns in Medieval Irish Narrative and Celtic Art*

Cross, T., and Slover. H., (1936) *Ancient Irish Tales*

Electronic Dictionary of the Irish Language, eDIL, (n.d.) Retrieved from http://edil.qub.ac.uk/dictionary/search.php

Fraser, J., (1915) *The First Battle of Moytura*

Gulermovich Epstein, A., (1998) *War Goddess: The Morrígan and her Germano-Celtic Counterparts*. Electronic version,#148, September, 1998. Retrieved from http://web.archive.org/web/20010616084231/members.loop.com/~musofire/diss/

Gray, E. (1983) *Cath Maige Tuired*

Green, M., (1992) *Dictionary of Celtic Myth and Legend*

Green, M., (1992) *Animals in Celtic Life and Myth*

Gregory, A., (1904) *Gods and Fighting Men*

Gwynn (1924) *The Metrical Dindshenchas*

Harper, D., (2014) *Danube*. Retrieved from http://www.etymon line.com/index.php?term=Danube&allowed_in_frame=0

Heijda, K., (2007) *War Goddesses, Furies, and Scald Crows*. University of Utrecht

Hennessey, WM. (1870) *The Ancient Irish Goddess of War.* Retrieved from http://www.sacred-texts.com/neu/celt/aigw/index.htm

Jones, M., (2009) *Anu.* Retrieved from http://www.mary jones.us/jce/anu.html

Jones, M., (2008) *Macha.* Retrieved from http://www.maryjones.us/jce/macha.html

Jones, M., (2014) *Táin Bó Regamna.* Retrieved from http://www.maryjones.us/ctexts/regamna.html

Jones, M., (2014) *Aided Conculaind.* Retrieved from http://www.maryjones.us/ctexts/cuchulain3.html

Keating, G., (1908) *The History of Ireland.* Retrieved from http://www.ucc.ie/celt/online/T100054/

Koch, J., (2005) *Celtic Culture, a Historical Encyclopedia*

Kondratiev, A., (1998) *Danu and Bile – Primordial Parents?* Retrieved from http://www.imbas.org/articles/danu_bile.html

Lambert, K., (2014) *The Irish War Goddesses.* Retrieved from http://dunsgathan.net/caithream/warGoddesses.html

Macalister, R. (1941) *Lebor Gabala Erenn*, volume IV

MacCulloch, J. (1911) *The Religion of the Ancient Celts.*

MacCulloch, J. (1918) *Celtic Mythology*

MacKillop, J., (1998) *Dictionary of Celtic Mythology*

Matthews, J., (1999) *Celtic Seers Sourcebook*

McCormick, F., (2008) *The Decline of the Cow: Agricultural and Settlement Change in Early Medieval Ireland*

McNeill, M., (1962) *Festival of Lughnasa*

Meyers, K., (1906) *The Triads of Ireland.* http://www.ucc.ie/celt/online/T103006.html

Monaghan, P., (2004) *An Encyclopedia of Irish Mythology and Folklore*

O Donaill (1977) *Focloir Gaeilge-Bearla*

O hOgain, D., (2006) *The Lore of Ireland*

O hOgain, D., (1995) *Irish Superstitions*

O'Rahilly, C., (2001) *Táin Bó Cúalnge Recension 1.* Retrieved from http://www.ucc.ie/celt/published/T301012/index.html

Puuvel, J., (1981) "Aspects of Equine Functionality"

Sjoestedt, M. (2000) *Celtic Gods and Heroes*

Smyth, D. (1988) *A Guide to Irish Mythology*

Squire, C. (2000) *The Mythology of the British Islands: An Introduction to Celtic Myth, Legend, Poetry and Romance*

Stokes, W., (1891) *Second Battle of Moytura*

Woodfield, S., (2011) *Celtic Lore & Spellcraft of the Dark Goddess: Invoking the Morrigan*

Wright, T., (1913) *The Historical Works of Giraldus Cambrensis*

Endnotes

1. Anu and Anand or Anann are the same name just as Danu and Danand or Danann are the same name. The difference between the –u ending and –nn ending is created by the case that the name is in when written in Irish Gaelic. Also at some point the Old Irish ending –nd shifted to a double –nn creating the change from Anand to Anann. So while the names look different and can seem confusing to English speakers the two sets represent different versions of two single names. In English these are most commonly given as Anu and Danu, respectively.

2. A prohibition of silence regarding an Otherworldly spouse is not an uncommon theme in fairylore. Generally such spouses will have some unusual rule that the human spouse must follow, and if broken the fairy returns immediately back from whence they came.

3. Halidom means a sacred place or thing.

4. Beannighe – the washer-at-the-ford type fairy.

5. Versicles are short chants or songs.

6. Danu is from the Celtic root Danu(w)yo from the proto-Indo-European Danu meaning river (Harper, 2014).

7. I recommend Michelle Skye's series of books, *Goddess Alive*, *Goddess Afoot*, and *Goddess Aloud* for some good guided meditations, several of which deal with the Morrigans, if you are interested.

8. After being offered and left on the altar during the ritual it is later given to the crows outside.

**MOON
BOOKS**

PAGANISM & SHAMANISM

What is Paganism? A religion, a spirituality, an alternative belief
system, nature worship? You can find support for all these
definitions (and many more) in dictionaries, encyclopaedias,
and text books of religion, but subscribe to any one and the
truth will evade you. Above all Paganism is a creative pursuit,
an encounter with reality, an exploration of meaning and an
expression of the soul. Druids, Heathens, Wiccans and others, all
contribute their insights and literary riches to the Pagan
tradition. Moon Books invites you to begin or to deepen your
own encounter, right here, right now.
If you have enjoyed this book, why not tell other readers by
posting a review on your preferred book site.

Recent bestsellers from Moon Books are:

Journey to the Dark Goddess
How to Return to Your Soul
Jane Meredith
Discover the powerful secrets of the Dark Goddess and
transform your depression, grief and pain into healing
and integration.
Paperback: 978-1-84694-677-6 ebook: 978-1-78099-223-5

Shamanic Reiki
Expanded Ways of Working with Universal Life Force Energy
Llyn Roberts, Robert Levy
Shamanism and Reiki are each powerful ways of healing;
together, their power multiplies. Shamanic Reiki introduces
techniques to help healers and Reiki practitioners tap ancient
healing wisdom.
Paperback: 978-1-84694-037-8 ebook: 978-1-84694-650-9

Pagan Portals – The Awen Alone
Walking the Path of the Solitary Druid
Joanna van der Hoeven
An introductory guide for the solitary Druid, The Awen Alone
will accompany you as you explore, and seek out your own
place within the natural world.
Paperback: 978-1-78279-547-6 ebook: 978-1-78279-546-9

A Kitchen Witch's World of Magical Herbs & Plants
Rachel Patterson
A journey into the magical world of herbs and plants, filled with
magical uses, folklore, history and practical magic. By popular
writer, blogger and kitchen witch, Tansy Firedragon.
Paperback: 978-1-78279-621-3 ebook: 978-1-78279-620-6

Medicine for the Soul
The Complete Book of Shamanic Healing
Ross Heaven
All you will ever need to know about shamanic healing and how
to become your own shaman...
Paperback: 978-1-78099-419-2 ebook: 978-1-78099-420-8

Shaman Pathways – The Druid Shaman
Exploring the Celtic Otherworld
Danu Forest
A practical guide to Celtic shamanism with exercises and
techniques as well as traditional lore for exploring the Celtic
Otherworld.
Paperback: 978-1-78099-615-8 ebook: 978-1-78099-616-5

Traditional Witchcraft for the Woods and Forests
A Witch's Guide to the Woodland with Guided Meditations and
Pathworking
Mélusine Draco
A Witch's guide to walking alone in the woods, with guided
meditations and pathworking.
Paperback: 978-1-84694-803-9 ebook: 978-1-84694-804-6

Naming the Goddess
Trevor Greenfield
Naming the Goddess is written by over eighty adherents and
scholars of Goddess and Goddess Spirituality.
Paperback: 978-1-78279-476-9 ebook: 978-1-78279-475-2

Shapeshifting into Higher Consciousness
Heal and Transform Yourself and Our World with Ancient
Shamanic and Modern Methods
Llyn Roberts
Ancient and modern methods that you can use every day to
transform yourself and make a positive difference in the world.
Paperback: 978-1-84694-843-5 ebook: 978-1-84694-844-2

Readers of ebooks can buy or view any of these bestsellers by
clicking on the live link in the title. Most titles are published in
paperback and as an ebook. Paperbacks are available in traditional bookshops. Both print and ebook formats are available
online.

Find more titles and sign up to our readers' newsletter at
http://www.johnhuntpublishing.com/paganism
Follow us on Facebook at
https://www.facebook.com/MoonBooks
and Twitter at https://twitter.com/MoonBooksJHP